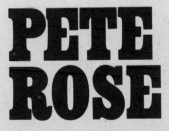

PETE ROSE

An inside look at one of baseball's greatest stars—the man they call "Charlie Hustle."

PETE ROSE

by Bob Rubin

illustrated with photographs

MAJOR LEAGUE
LIBRARY

RANDOM HOUSE · NEW YORK

Library of Congress Cataloging in Publication Data
Rubin, Bob.   Pete Rose.   (Major league library)
SUMMARY: A biography stressing the baseball career of the star outfielder of the Cincinnati Reds, Pete Rose.
1. Rose, Pete, 1942–   —Juvenile literature.   2. Baseball—Juvenile literature. [1. Rose, Pete, 1942–   2. Baseball—Biography]   I. Title.
GV865.R65R82   796.357′092′4 [B] [92]   74–24761
ISBN 0–394–83026–1   ISBN 0–394–93026–6 lib. bdg.

Manufactured in the United States of America   1 2 3 4 5 6 7 8 9 0

PHOTOGRAPH CREDITS: Clifton Boutelle, 2–3, 99; Ken Regan (Camera 5), 98; United Press International, endpapers, 5, 7, 22, 23 (both), 24, 25 (both), 26, 38, 39, 61, 62 (both), 63, 65, 85, 86, 87, 97 (both), 111, 112 top, 125, 126, 127, 137, 138, 139, 140, 148; Wide World Photos, 37, 64, 112 bottom, 124.

COVER: Photo by Malcolm Emmons

To
Teddy, Larry and Bonnie,
co-workers and friends . . .
to cousin Steve, Aunt Bette
and Uncle Norman, Iris,
Herb, Randy and Ma Freda . . .
to Gypso, Dipso and the
two Nipsos, Bobby and Ron,
Jane and Bobby . . . to Sam,
Ali and Fang . . . and, as
always, my Penny

I have drawn on many sources in the course of writing this book. I would like to thank Jim Ferguson and Bob Rathgeber of the Cincinnati Reds for their cooperation. Two books, *The Pete Rose Story* by Pete Rose and *Pete Rose: They Call Him "Charlie Hustle"* by Bill Libby, provided valuable information, as did magazine stories by Berry Stainback, Maury Allen, Paul Hemphill, Vic Zeigel, John Devaney and Dick Kaplan and numerous newspaper stories by Earl Lawson.

RR

CONTENTS

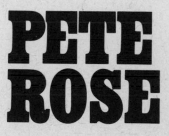

THEY
CALL HIM
"CHARLIE
HUSTLE"

"Other guys give one hundred percent. I have to give one hundred and ten percent."

It was the bottom of the twelfth inning of the 1970 All-Star game. The 51,838 spectators jammed into Cincinnati's new Riverfront Stadium began their familiar rhythmic clapping as right fielder Pete Rose of the hometown Reds advanced to the plate. The score was tied 4–4, and the partisan National League crowd was counting on Rose to get something started. The stocky, barrel-chested Reds star certainly was due. Since entering the game back in the fifth inning, he had gone hitless in two at-bats, striking out both times.

Behind the plate for the American League was Cleveland catcher Ray Fosse. Just the night before, Rose, Fosse, and their wives had gone out to dinner together, then spent the evening at Rose's home.

11

There had been some good-natured joking about the upcoming All-Star game, with each man predicting a victory for his team.

Now Rose turned to his friend—and rival—and said, "Damn it, Ray, give me something I can at least foul tip. I haven't hit the ball yet."

Pitcher Clyde Wright threw twice. Rose intently watched both deliveries from the instant they were released until they thudded into Fosse's big mitt. Both were balls. Wright's third pitch never reached Fosse's glove, as Rose lined the fastball to center field for a single.

Dodger infielder Bill Grabarkewitz followed with another single, advancing Rose to second base. Then with two outs, Chicago's Jim Hickman lined another hit to center, setting up one of the most dramatic plays in the long, colorful history of baseball's All-Star game.

Off at the crack of Hickman's bat, Rose raced for third. Instinctively, he hit the inside of the bag with his right foot, turning sharply toward home rather than wasting precious steps by going wide.

The hard-hit ball was fielded cleanly by center fielder Amos Otis, who came up throwing. Sensing a close play at the plate, the cheering crowd suddenly hushed in anticipation.

Otis' throw screamed in from the outfield, flying directly over second base and the pitcher's mound on its swift path to Fosse's waiting glove. The American

League catcher was straddling the foul line a stride up toward third base as Rose came roaring down from third. His muscular legs churning, his face red and contorted, Pete labored to somehow squeeze an extra bit of speed out of his straining body. Last night's good time with the Fosses had vanished completely from his mind as he pounded for home. Now Fosse was simply an opponent—an obstacle standing between Pete and victory.

Rose reached Fosse a split-second before Otis' throw arrived. Like a football player hitting the line with third down and one yard to go, Rose lowered his head and hit the crouching catcher. At 6-foot-2 and 220 pounds, Fosse had three inches and 20 pounds on Rose. But the Red runner had all the momentum on his side, and that more than made up for his size disadvantage. As the two men collided, Fosse flew one way, Rose another, and the ball still another. In the jumble of flying bodies, Pete managed to reach out and slap the plate for the winning run. Fosse suffered a severe shoulder injury on the play and had to be helped into the American League locker room.

The fans stayed in place as if glued to their seats. Even after the roar died, a hum of excitement buzzed like an electric current. The play was the talk of both locker rooms.

"Fosse was a stride up the line," said Rose, "and had the baseline completely straddled. I started to slide, and I saw I couldn't make it. Head-first, it would have been worse. No way. I just had to run and hit him. I got him with the knee, the whole body, everything, and he was crouched. I thought I hit a mountain."

"Fosse was in the act of receiving it when Pete hit him," said National League manager Gil Hodges. "It was just a bit before the ball got to him, and it hit his glove or someplace. The boy had the plate blocked, and Pete was going to score one way or another."

Over on the losers' side, pitcher Clyde Wright was less philosophical. "Why in hell did Rose have to do it?" he demanded angrily. "I guess it's instinct. I guess that's how he plays. But from where I was standing, it looked like he could have gone around him."

Dick Dietz, the National League batter who was on deck when Rose scored, emphatically disagreed with Wright. "It was the only play Pete had," he insisted. "Fosse had the plate blocked off with both feet spread."

Even Fosse wasn't sure that Rose could have avoided the contact and still scored. "Some guys on the bench thought he could have gone around me," the catcher said as he dressed with obvious pain for a trip to the hospital. "I don't know. It's the way he runs. He's got to score any way he can, I guess."

The final word belonged to Rose. "I don't want anybody to get hurt," he said. "Fosse is my friend. I started to slide, head-first. But if I slide, I get slaughtered. I'm trying to score. I got to win. He did his job. I did mine."

"I got to win!" If you had to sum up Pete Rose in one sentence, that would do fine. Never mind that the All-Star game, for all its glamor, is still only an exhibition that doesn't count in the standings. Never mind that many veterans privately admit they'd just as soon spend the three-day All-Star break at home relaxing with their families as play in what they consider a meaningless contest. To Pete Rose, there was no such thing as a meaningless game, and there was nothing he enjoyed more than playing baseball. And as Ray Fosse and hundreds of other ballplayers could testify, when Pete Rose played, he always played to win.

Peter Edward Rose was a rarity among modern ballplayers, a man whose love of the game was total and enduring. "The major leagues is my home," Pete once said. "It's all I've ever wanted to do in my life. I can't think of a single thing wrong with the game of baseball. It's clean and exciting, and it gives a guy like me a big chance to make a big man of himself. Every game is different; every season is different. No matter what you did, you've always got a chance to do it all over again.

"I have a beautiful wife and two fine children, and I'm able to give them a fine home and a good life because of baseball. I live in style, but I live the game.

On the road, I rarely leave the hotel room so I can save my legs for the game at night. I do what has to be done to be the best because I want to do it, because I want to be the best."

For most of his life, Pete worked hard to achieve that goal. He joined the Reds in 1963, and was a perennial All-Star almost from the start. Originally a second baseman, he was switched briefly to third in 1965, then moved permanently to the outfield. He became a fine outfielder with a respected throwing arm, but Rose's greatest weapon was always his bat.

In an era when .300 hitters were a rare breed, the switch-hitting Rose strung together nine consecutive .300 seasons. Three times in his first twelve major league years, he led the National League in hitting, and his career average of .310 ranked third among all active major leaguers.

In an era when getting 200 hits in a season was even rarer than batting .300, Rose enjoyed six years with 200 or more hits and just missed two others when he finished with 192 (1971) and 198 (1972). Basically a singles hitter, he had 2,337 hits at the end of 1974 and seemed a cinch to someday join the exclusive 3,000-hit club.

As impressive as his statistics were, however, it would be impossible to describe Rose as a ballplayer simply in terms of numbers. He played with a kind of energy and enthusiasm that made his statistics seem pale.

"I'm never satisfied," Rose once said. "I get a single, I want a double. I get a double, I want a triple. The idea of this game, it's not to get on base. The idea of this game is to score."

Rose's attitude earned him a nickname way back in his rookie year, one that stuck throughout his career. They called him "Charlie Hustle," and seldom has any athlete's nickname proved more appropriate. Former Yankee pitching star Whitey Ford gave Rose the name the first time he saw him in action. It was during spring training, and Rose had just drawn a base on balls. Ford watched in awe as Pete sprinted to first base as if he were trying to beat out a bunt.

"Running is the most natural thing in the world for me," explained Rose. "I guess I was born with all this nervous energy. I can't sit still. I never could go trout fishing or squirrel hunting, or anything like that. You have to sit around and wait too darned long. Some say baseball is slow; but if the player works at it there's always something he can do to speed things along. I work at it, but it comes natural. Hustle is something that's born in you. Sure, I suppose you can make any guy hustle tomorrow, but most of the guys won't still be hustling next week. It's either in you or it's not.

"A lot of things we do are habits. If you learn to run hard, to hustle no matter what you're doing on a ballfield, it carries over to everything you do on the field. If you learn to save yourself here and there, pretty soon you're doing a lot of things half-speed. I learned to hustle early. Now it's a habit. A lot of people think it's an act, but it's something that comes natural to me."

To spot Pete Rose in a hurry, all his fans had to do was look for the ballplayer with the dirty uniform—dirty from diving head-long after a ball in the field or diving into a base to beat a throw. "People ask me why I slide on my stomach instead of putting on one of those fancy feet-first hook slides," Pete said. "I slide on my stomach because it's faster. Maybe it hurts more, but what's hurting? Anyway, you can break your ankle or your leg a lot faster than you can your belly or your arm. And I don't want to miss any games. I don't want to miss anything."

In 1971, *Sport* magazine asked 30 major leaguers to name their choice for the title of "Baseball's Greatest Competitor." The players polled listed eight attributes baseball's greatest competitor should possess: consistency, ability in the clutch, tenacity, flair, ability to inspire, pride, team play, and love of the game. Based on those standards, the man they picked, by a huge margin, was Pete Rose.

"People talk about 'natural talent,' " Lou Brock, the great base-stealing star of the St. Louis Cardinals, told *Sport*. "What is 'natural talent?' Every guy that reaches the big leagues has 'natural talent,' but how many stay there? The difference is in competitiveness."

When it came to competitiveness, no one could deny that Pete was number one. Here are some of the things managers, teammates, and opponents have said about Charlie Hustle.

Former Cincinnati shortstop Woody Woodward: "When I first saw him, I couldn't believe the guy. He doesn't stop. On the field, he goes all the time. And he's the same off the field as he is on it. Everything is go, go, go. On the bus to and from the ballpark he can't sit still. He's walking up and down the aisle or standing in the doorway waiting to get out. On the plane flights, he helps the stewardesses serve the other players their meals."

Former Cincinnati second baseman Tommy Helms, Rose's ex-roommate: "I wake up one morning about the break of dawn and I see my roomie in his pajamas in a batting crouch. I ask him what in the heck he's doing. And he said, 'I'm working on my batting. You're ahead of me, Rook' (I was a rookie then). 'A veteran like me can't let a rook get ahead of him. I got to catch up. I got to catch up.' He's always saying he's got to catch up to something. And even after he caught me and passed me, he's still up at the break of dawn swinging an imaginary bat. I've never seen anyone with so damn much enthusiasm and so damn much energy. Just being with him gets you tired."

Reds' manager Sparky Anderson: "When it's hot and other players are getting weaker, Pete is getting stronger. He plays every game, runs all the time, and means it when he says, 'I hope it's a hundred and ten degrees because the pitcher will feel it more than I will.' He's like an animal . . .

"And when I want to try to figure which pitchers we might face at, say, New York in ten days, I just ask Pete. He'll rattle off the rotation we're likely to face, and he's rarely wrong."

Reds' coach Alex Grammas: "Pete isn't ashamed to tell everyone that baseball made him what he is today. Sure, a lot of other guys making big money might say the same thing, but not with Pete's enthusiasm. He makes no bones about it. You never hear him knocking the game. He talks it the way he plays it. What I mean is, he plays the game with hustle and talks about it with enthusiasm."

Montreal Expos' manager Gene Mauch: "Pete Rose is the kind of ballplayer every manager likes to manage. He's not afraid to get tired or dirty. He's proud of the things he can do well. He's proud of being the game's top hustler, and he goes out to try to prove every day that his reputation is justified."

Former Reds' manager Dave Bristol: "Rose comes to play ball. One spring he pulled a muscle and the doctor told him to rest three or four days. We had to hide his uniform. Hide it! If we didn't, he'd be in it and on the field begging to play."

Former Reds' official Phil Seghi, who signed Rose to his first pro contract: "You always want to know what's inside a boy when you sign him, but you really can't see inside to know if there is purpose and desire and dedication and ambition. But with Pete, you didn't have to look inside him. He oozed all these things."

And as Reds' general manager Bob Howsam put it: "Pete would run over his mother to get another time at bat!"

Living up to his nickname—Charlie Hustle—Rose crashes into American League catcher Ray Fosse to score the winning run in the 1970 All-Star game (opposite). A moment later he watches anxiously as Fosse writhes in pain (above), and after the game he takes a well-earned rest in the locker room.

Pete shows more of his competitive fire. At left, he slides across the plate after knocking over Giant catcher Doug Rader, who had the ball but missed the tag. Above, Pete climbs a wall in a vain attempt to catch the ball, and at right he races home to score on a sacrifice fly.

Rose's will to win gets out of hand in a 1969 game. Catcher Johnny Bench and Reds manager Dave Bristol have to restrain him in an argument with the umpires.

LIKE FATHER, LIKE SON

"Some kids are raised on rice and potatoes. I was raised on athletics."

PETE ROSE

Whoever first said "Like father, like son" could have been talking about Harry "Pete" Rose and his son Pete. "He made me into the ballplayer I am," said Pete. "They call me Charlie Hustle, and I'm proud they do. But you know who taught me to hustle? My dad. He believed that the best way, the only way to win was to be competitive, to drive, to try your hardest every single minute. My father was the most important guy in my life."

Harry Rose was a bank cashier and one of the greatest sandlot athletes in Cincinnati when Pete was born on April 14, 1942. The elder Rose boxed in his youth, played semi-pro baseball until he was 38, and was a semi-pro football player until the age of 42. He and Pete's mother met at a baseball game.

28

Harry Rose was strong and tough, and that's the way he wanted his son to be. "When I started to play football, my dad didn't want me to wear a face guard," Pete recalled. "You know how kids in high school wear teeth guards? When he heard about that, he said, 'A teeth guard! Are you kidding me?' My father watched pro football on television. He'd get mad when a player would call for a fair catch. He'd say, 'He could get one yard, and how many times does a team miss a touchdown by one yard!' They used to say if you tackled my father low, he kicked you, and if you tackled him high, he straight-armed you in the teeth. But he wasn't a dirty player."

Pete remembered one football game where he watched his father kick off, suffer a broken hip from a hard block as he raced downfield, and then try to *crawl* after the ballcarrier in an attempt to make the tackle. "That was the kind of man he was," Pete said proudly. "He was always a head-knocker. Man, was he a head-knocker."

As a child, Pete tagged along whenever his dad had a game. "When he played baseball, I was the bat boy," recalled Rose. "When he played basketball, I was the ball boy. When he played football, I was the water boy. I probably wouldn't have been an athlete if I hadn't had a father like mine."

When Pete wasn't with his dad, he was usually playing ball with his friends or his younger brother Dave. The Roses lived in Anderson Ferry, a small river town a few miles west of Cincinnati.

Pete and his little brother used to play a game called houseball, bouncing a rubber ball off the brick walls of Schulte's, a restaurant in Anderson Ferry. They'd play there all day and into the night, with Pete's brother pitching to Pete. As Pete grew, his brother would move closer so his pitches would appear faster. "We played so much houseball against that old red brick building that I think we wore the paint away," Pete recalled years later.

Life was free and easy for the Rose boys. They would find and return empty soda bottles, collecting a pocketful of change, or snitch watermelons from a farmer's field. Pete's favorite activities were riding on the ferryboats, camping out in the steep Ohio hills, or just playing around on the riverbank. More often than not, though, he'd be at the parking lot at Schulte's, playing houseball and pretending he was a member of the Cincinnati Reds.

"I grew up attending every game the Cincinnati Reds played," Pete explained. "When my dad didn't lug me out to the ballpark, I would sit at home, glued to the radio, tuned in on the action. School days were a different matter, but there you are. And when I wasn't attending the baseball games in person or by radio, I was playing in them—in my imagination, of course."

Although baseball was Pete's first love, it wasn't his only one. Constantly encouraged by his father, he played all sports. When Pete was just three, his dad went out to buy Pete's sister Jackie a pair of shoes. But when he came back, he was carrying a pair of miniature boxing gloves for Pete instead. "Mom nearly had a fit," Rose said.

Years later, Pete actually fought a few amateur bouts in which he displayed characteristic Rose spunk. "He was a whale of a competitor," said one coach who remembered him. "You could see he would be something special, no matter what his main sport was. The last time he fought, he was only fifteen—he'd lied about his age to get into the action—and he'd only had two or three fights. He fought a veteran amateur named Candy Jamison, who was about thirty and must have had two hundred fights. Well, Candy was too smart, but Petey chased him all over the ring before the decision went against him."

"I beat him, but they gave the decision to the other guy," said Pete, who never liked to lose at anything.

Boxing was fun, but baseball was still Pete's number one interest. Between playing it and watching it, he picked up many tips that would eventually make him a pro. In fact, Pete got the inspiration to hustle anytime he was on the field after witnessing a contest at Cincinnati's old Crosley Field with his father.

"We were watching the Reds play the Cardinals," Pete recalled, "and Enos Slaughter of the Cards got a base on balls. Slaughter raced down to first as if he were trying to beat out a bunt. Dad said to me, 'That's the way to play baseball, Pete. It wouldn't hurt you to do something like that, because a little hustle can make up for a lot of mistakes.' "

Pete began his organized baseball career as a nine-year-old catcher for the Sedamsville Civic Club's Knot Hole Gang. The day Pete played his first game for that team was the day Harry Rose gave up his active sports career. That gave him more time than ever to devote to his son's game. Although Pete was only a young boy then, his father and his uncle Buddy Bloebaum (a Cincinnati Reds' scout and a former minor leaguer) were already dreaming of a possible major league future for him.

With that future in mind the two older men had advised Pete to be a catcher. "There are fewer good catchers in professional baseball than anything else," Bloebaum explained.

Probably the most important thing his two "coaches" decided that year was that Pete, a natural right-hander, should learn to switch-hit. As his uncle Buddy explained, there are two advantages to switch-hitting.

First of all, batting lefty puts a hitter two steps closer to first base and thus enables him to beat out some grounders that a righty might miss by a stride. Second, a switch-hitter never has to master curveballs that look like they're coming straight at his head, then break over the plate at the last instant. A switch-hitter always bats left-handed against a right-handed pitcher and vice versa, so breaking pitches always start outside and curve in toward him.

"It's been a big help to me, there's no doubt of that," Pete said years later. "At first I wasn't too good left-handed, of course, but Dad made me stay with it until I got good at it. I remember when I was going into the Knot Hole League—the Cincinnati equivalent of Little League ball in those days—Dad went up to my manager and struck a bargain with him. The only way Dad would let me play, he said, was if the manager let me switch-hit.

"Dad understood that he was asking a lot. 'I realize that you might run into a championship game facing a right-handed pitcher,' he told the manager, 'but I want Pete to bat left-handed against every right-hander, no matter what. I want your word you'll let him switch. He'll probably be weak left-handed, but if you want Pete to play for you all summer, he's got to be a switcher.' "

The manager agreed and from then on Pete Rose was a switch-hitter.

Years later, Pete realized that through him, his dad was living the life he would have loved to live had he had the opportunity. It's a situation that can lead to terrific strain between father and son if the son is unwilling—or unable—to make his father's dream come true. But in the case of the Roses, there was no such conflict. Both wanted the same thing for Pete and, fortunately, Pete had the talent to reach their goal.

Harry Rose had once dreamed of becoming a major leaguer himself. Pete often thought how unfair it was that his father was never able to fulfill his own ambitions but had to be content to see them realized by his son.

In his own youth, Pete's father had been so busy studying and working after school that he didn't have the time to even watch his high school football team, much less play on it. "That's one reason I always kept hustling," Pete explained. "I had to give my dad, through me, all the moments he never had time for when he was a kid. If I didn't hustle out there, I'd be letting him down something awful."

Harry Rose tried to hammer all he knew about baseball into his young son's head, and Pete was more than willing to learn. For hours on end Mr. Rose had Pete practice batting left-handed and, above all, he constantly reminded his son how important it was to keep his eye on the ball no matter which way he was hitting. "Never take your eyes off the ball, Pete," he would repeat over and over until Pete heard it in his sleep.

During their frequent father-son batting practices, Pete might be ready and eager to hit, but Harry Rose would hold the ball, moving it from side to side, sometimes for several minutes. If at any point Pete's attention wandered for even a fraction of a second, his dad would say, "Okay, Pete, you're not looking."

It was a lesson Pete never forgot. Even as a big leaguer he always watched the ball until it disappeared into the catcher's mitt, explaining that pitches that look bad halfway to the plate often have an embarrassing way of turning into strikes at the very last second. "The only sure way to know," he said, "is to keep your eye on the ball."

All that expert coaching made nine-year-old Pete a stand-out in his first year with the Sedamsville team. More than 20 years later, Pete still remembered his first season of baseball. One of his favorite memories concerned the jackets he and his teammates were given at the end of the season for winning a championship. "Those jackets were beauties. I know because I wanted to sleep in mine. I wore it everywhere. That's how much I loved it," Rose said years later.

Pete also reminisced about his grandfather, who had been dying of cancer that year. The old man lived in Sedamsville and spent most of his time playing solitaire and entertaining his grandson with tales of his own baseball prowess as a youngster. As Pete recalled, "He was forever telling me about the time he hit a baseball so hard that it sailed clear out of Bold Face Park, cleared the railroad yards, and landed on the river where it hit a sternwheel steamboat, causing the boat to sink."

Although the old man was deathly ill at the time,

he insisted on attending the game when Pete's Knot Hole Gang team played for the championship at Bold Face Park. Pete never forgot the sight of his grandfather standing with the support of Pete's dad, shielding his eyes from the sun and watching Pete take part in his first championship effort.

The following year (1952) Pete caught and played a little third base for the Delhi Eagles, one of several boys' teams he joined as he worked his way through different age group leagues. In 1955 he entered Western Hills High School. "I was the sports addict from Anderson Ferry," he recalled. "I went out for everything but the girls' swimming team."

During spring training in 1974, Pete gets a visit from his family: his daughter Fawn Renee, his wife Karolyn and his son Pete, Jr.

Three generations of Roses: Pete's father, Harry "Pete" Rose, above left;
Pete; and young Pete Rose, Jr., far right.

GROWING UP

"It scares me to think of the kids I see now—the dropouts—hanging around street corners these days, forever on the edge of things. Any one of them could have been me. I was that close to flushing everything down the drain."

PETE ROSE

Pete played guard for the Western Hills freshman basketball team, halfback for the football team, and caught for the baseball team. "I was having a ball," he said. "It seemed like everything was going my way. I figured I had the world by the tail." Pete's happiness was short-lived, however. In his sophomore year the 130-pound youngster was judged too small to play varsity football. To Rose, it was a catastrophe of major proportions—one he just couldn't handle.

As an adult, Pete looked back at that year with dismay. "I did a lot of dumb things that I regret even today," he said.

He'd skip school entirely, or go for just a half day. He and some fellow truants would go to the movies or just loaf, each feeling sorry for himself over some injustice, real or imaginary.

41

The little time Pete did spend in school wasn't much more productive. He'd fool around, or he'd dawdle and be late to class, or he'd get into a fight. "For a while that year, I spent more time in the assistant principal's office than I did in class," he recalled.

Pete was mixed up and miserable. Frustrated at seeing classmates playing ball when he could not, he even ignored his father's frequent warnings and lectures. Finally, he flunked his sophomore year.

"Simple as that," he admitted. "I goofed up completely. About the only thing I got a good grade in was gym. But what good is an A in gym when the rest of the grades would be nothings? Listen, that year I even flunked study hall—or if they had given a grade in it I would have flunked it. Yeah, I was a real winner."

Still a sophomore the following year Pete was delighted to find that he had grown enough to play football. He was the right halfback on a team that finished with a 7–2–1 record and won a share of the Public School championship.

Pete never played varsity basketball, so he spent an impatient few months after the football season waiting for the start of baseball. Meanwhile, he did just enough studying to stay in school. When the baseball season finally began, however, Pete was more than willing to learn everything he could about the game. A fine second baseman and a versatile hitter, Rose dedicated himself to constant improvement on the field. When the high school season ended, he simply continued playing in a summer league.

"I never even had a vacation," he said. "Dad thought it would hurt my future to take me away from the game and my team's summers, so I kept at it. And I didn't mind. I enjoyed it. I was good at it. When I wasn't practicing with my team, I was out in the backyard swinging against my dad's pitching."

"We never asked him to work summers," Harry Rose once recalled. "He never had a job. Sports was his only job growing up. But he did the job right."

Pete was ineligible to play high school baseball as a senior because it was his fifth year in high school. Instead, he played second base for Lebanon in the Daytona Amateur League and batted a cool .500. The Reds had a special program for hot young local prospects, so Pete and several other high school stars got the opportunity to work out with them at Crosley Field on late spring afternoons when the Reds team was playing night games. There stood young Pete in a Reds uniform, shagging flies while such stars as Frank Robinson, Vada Pinson and Gus Bell took batting practice. To Pete and his father it was like a dream come true.

"The first afternoon Pete was down there, I rushed out to the ballpark as soon as I got off from work," Harry Rose recalled. "I didn't know then about getting in at the pass gate. I went to the front and asked the ticket seller how soon I could get into the park. He said they didn't open till six. And Pete had been there since four. So I paced up and down until six, went in, and there was Pete—in uniform. I choked up. You know, there was my boy in uniform . . . I felt that if Pete never took another step in baseball, at least I had seen him in a major league uniform."

Pete experienced another memorable first at the end of his senior year of high school. As a graduation present, his mother gave him money to buy his first car. "Does every guy fall in love with his first car?" Pete wondered. "I know I did. I bought it for a hundred bucks. It was a 1937 Plymouth with no front bumper. It had a radio and a stick shift. It was dark blue. And it only had 35,000 miles on it. But it looked so funny without that front bumper that when I brought it home my mother looked out the window and laughed. Even though it had running boards, she kept laughing because she couldn't believe that I paid a hundred bucks for it."

Pete was so happy with his new wheels, that he decided to drive over and impress a girl he knew instead of working out at Crosley Field. His father, waiting impatiently at the ballpark, called home and asked his mother where Pete was.

"I think he said something about going over to a girl's house after school," Mrs. Rose replied.

"Do you know their number?" Harry Rose asked.

"Well, call him, and tell him to get the hell to the ballpark."

"Forty-five minutes later, there I was in uniform, chasing flies," Rose recalled with a sheepish grin.

Pete's hot bat and fiery hustle in the Daytona League did not go unnoticed. Jack Baker, a friend of Pete's uncle Buddy Bloebaum and a scout for the Baltimore Orioles, watched Pete pound out five hits in five at-bats in one game, turned to Bloebaum and said, "I'm having our head scout come out and look at Pete the first chance he gets. Make sure the kid doesn't do anything till he hears from Baltimore."

But Bloebaum, a scout for the Reds, had other ideas about Pete's future. On the night Pete graduated from high school, Pete's uncle paid his father a surprise visit. It was a surprise because Bloebaum was supposed to be in a distant town named Piqua to help conduct a clinic for the Reds.

"I thought you were in Piqua," said Pete's father.

"Well, I'm not," replied his uncle. "Got more important things to do."

"Like what?" asked Harry Rose.

"About Pete's future."

"But he's not here. He's out celebrating. You know how kids are on graduation night."

"Let's give him a little more to celebrate when he gets home. The Reds want to talk to him about a contract."

"When?"

"Tomorrow morning."

Exhilarated at the prospect of signing with the team he had rooted for since boyhood, Pete was in the Crosley Field executive offices early the next morning with his father and uncle.

However, before going inside, Pete and his dad took a walk on the field. Neither said much. Both were lost in thought over the momentous event that was looming ahead, the fulfillment of both men's dreams.

"Suddenly, I felt like maybe I was really a part of it," Pete recalled, "not just a kid from high school out there catching flies on schoolday afternoons with a bunch of other guys. That old park never looked better than it did that morning.

The Reds offered Rose a $7,000 bonus for signing plus an extra $5,000 if he lasted on the major league roster for at least 30 days. But Harry Rose said he had promised the Orioles he'd speak to them before Pete signed with anyone else, even though uncle Buddy warned, "A bird in the hand is worth two Orioles in the bush."

Pete didn't say anything while the older men discussed his future. But inside, he was ready to explode. "Goodbye $7,000," he recalled thinking. "Goodbye Cincinnati Reds. A bird in the hand is worth ten zillion Orioles in the bush. That's what I wanted to say."

Harry Rose may have sensed Pete's emotions, for

suddenly he turned to his son. "Listen," he said softly, "I shouldn't be making this decision at all. Pete, what do you think?"

With no hesitation, Pete spoke up loud and clear. "I'd like to sign," he said.

There was still another decision to be made that day. Pete would report to the Reds' Class D minor league team in Geneva, New York. The only question was when.

Reds' official Phil Seghi offered Pete two choices. He could report to Geneva immediately and start to play right away, or he could wait around until the following spring and begin his professional career in Tampa.

Seghi warned Pete that he would face a rough adjustment if he went to Geneva. He pointed out that even though Pete had been playing sandlot ball three times a week, he really wasn't in shape for the rugged playing and traveling schedule he'd find in pro ball. He also warned Pete that the players with whom he'd be competing would be light years better than those he'd starred against in Daytona.

It didn't matter. Seghi could have told Pete they'd be throwing knives at him instead of baseballs and it wouldn't have changed Rose's mind.

"Dumb me," Pete recalled. "I said, 'I want to go right now.'"

"At least wait until Monday," Seghi said with a grin. "That's when the plane leaves."

48

The two-day wait until Monday seemed like forever to Pete. But finally he was on the runway. "Moments later Cincinnati was spread out before me as far as the eye could see," Rose recalled. "The last thing I saw before we vanished into the clouds and haze was that most beautiful of all sights: the Cincinnati Reds' baseball park. Then once above the clouds, I turned my attention to the future."

THE
MINOR
LEAGUES

"Some of the stuff tore your heart out and some of the stuff made you grow up fast. Lots of times you behaved like a bunch of kids on the first day of summer vacation. I spent two-and-one-half years in that apprenticeship. It was the greatest apprenticeship a guy could have."

PETE ROSE

Class D was the lowest minor league in all of pro ball. The Reds, like all the other major league teams, started their prospects in the low minors as the first step on the ladder up, hopefully to the majors. Still, the caliber of baseball played by the Geneva Reds was far superior to anything Pete had known. Now he would be competing against some of the very best young baseball players in the country. All of them had also been high school and sandlot stars. To make things even more difficult, Pete was joining the team months after the start of the season, so he was probably the least experienced player in the whole league.

Actually, life wasn't easy for any of the players in Class D. The stadiums were old and rickety, and the fields weren't in any better shape. The buses that transported teams to road games were just about ready for the junk heap, and the rides often lasted many muscle-aching hours. When Pete came to Geneva in 1960, the meal allowance was three dollars per day, so he and his teammates practically lived on hamburgers. But the only thing that really bothered Pete was loneliness.

Geneva was about 500 miles from Anderson Ferry and everything that was familiar to Pete. "That was the farthest I had ever been away from home," he recalled. "And I will be the first to admit I was probably the lonesomest and most homesick guy that Geneva ever had."

To make things worse, the Geneva fans and ballplayers were hardly waiting to welcome Pete. Word had gotten around that a "star" from the parent Reds' hometown was on the way. Not surprisingly, the Geneva players resented the newcomer's advance buildup.

Before long, Pete's teammates had another reason to resent the newcomer. The club management decided to use Pete at second base, shifting the regular second baseman, a popular prospect named Tony Perez, to third. That didn't exactly endear Pete to the Geneva fans or his new teammates, even though he'd had no say at all about the switch of positions. Perez was one of several Cubans on the Geneva team who mostly spoke to each other in Spanish, so there wasn't much Rose could say to him. (Years later, Rose and Perez both starred with the major league club.)

But Pete refused to let anything get him down. He loved baseball, and now he was actually getting paid to play. Nothing else really mattered. Soon his enthusiasm for the game and his natural friendliness overcame his teammates' reservations, and by the end of the season he was actually voted the team's most popular player.

On the field, however, Rose's efforts were less successful. His fielding was erratic (he led the league in errors with a whopping 36 in 85 games). Surprisingly, he had even more trouble batting. Until he began to adjust to the superior pro pitching he was now facing, his hitting was almost nonexistent. In short, Rose was learning the differences between amateur and professional baseball—the hard way.

Pete did all he could to improve, taking extra batting practice and fielding thousands of grounders during infield drills. Still, his progress was slow. One night Pete's father visited the team when it was playing in Erie, Pennsylvania, and privately asked the Geneva manager how his son was doing. He was stunned to hear the manager reel off a long list of criticisms.

Harry Rose recalled that in the span of just a few minutes he was told "five thousand" things that were wrong with Pete. Finally, he lamely suggested the manager try Pete as a catcher, and then the conversation faded away. Wisely, Mr. Rose did not tell Pete what the manager had said. A young ballplayer's psyche is a delicate thing, and a blow to the ego can do a lot more damage than a fastball in the ribs.

Rose wound up a so-so first season of pro ball with a .277 batting average and immediately reported to the Winter Instructional League in Florida for more work. That winter he could have been drafted cheap by any other major league team, but none found him worth even a small investment. Harry Rose managed to get a look at the major league scouting report on Pete and was depressed to read, "Pete Rose can't make a double play, can't throw, can't hit left-handed, and can't run."

But despite the gloom and doom, Rose did have some admirers. One was a young Reds' prospect, Chico Ruiz, who told reporters in Florida, "That Rose, he's got a line-drive bat."

More important for Pete's future, Reds' manager Fred Hutchinson saw something in the spunky, barrel-chested youngster. The manager was especially impressed with the tremendous enthusiasm with which Pete played the game. "That kid's going to make it in a hurry," Hutchinson told Reds' general manager Gabe Paul. "He won't need too much grooming. This kid likes to play."

At Hutchinson's suggestion, Pete was jumped from Class D to the Reds' Class A Tampa team in the Florida State League for the 1961 season.

By the time he reported to Tampa for spring training, the "kid" was a rock-hard 194-pound man. The increased weight was all muscle—a fringe benefit of Rose's off-season job loading boxcars for Railway Express. His added strength and stamina made Pete a better all-round ballplayer, as he proved dramatically that season.

Pete played 130 games with the Tampa team and hit .331, leading the league in hits (160) and triples (30) and scoring 105 runs. He also reduced his number of errors to 21 and greatly improved his execution of the double play. In fact, Pete did so well there that he won the league's Player of the Year award.

Rose had another great season in '62, playing for Macon of the Class A Sally League. He picked up right where he'd left off in Tampa, belting out hits left and right. His frantic dashes around the bases, his dramatic head-first slides and his always-dirty uniform earned him the nickname "Hollywood."

Macon manager Dave Bristol, who became manager of the Cincinnati Reds in 1966, didn't quite know what to make of his cocky young hot shot. "The first time I saw Rose, I kind of sat back and watched him running all the time to everywhere," Bristol recalled with a smile. "I asked myself, 'Is he putting me on with all this razzmatazz, or is he real? Is it going to be like this all the time?' Well, it was. He never gave up all year—not once on anything."

Although Pete was having a fine season, not all of his teammates fared as well. Baseball is a business, and any player who doesn't have the talent to compete is simply dropped. Rose saw lots of young men whose dreams of baseball glory ended in the minors, but he never got used to it. "Probably the loneliest sight in the world," he said, "is to see a guy who has been released, killing time at the ballpark, watching the rest of us work out while he stands there in civvies, hanging onto his suitcase and waiting for the bus that will take him away from everything he'd ever dreamed of."

Rose made it a practice not to look at a man whose departure was imminent. It was too painful. "You get a gut feeling because there are no guarantees in baseball," he explained. He knew only too well the possibility that tomorrow it could be him standing there saying goodbye to a lifelong dream. Just the thought of it made Pete bear down even harder than ever.

Life in the minors wasn't always a grim struggle for survival, however. There were many light-hearted moments, and Pete enjoyed his share. For example, there was the time a station wagon full of Macon players, including Pete, were taking a long, boring ride to Charlotte, North Carolina. Rose, sitting on top of a pile of equipment in the back, finally decided to break the monotony. No one noticed as he quietly opened the back window. No one noticed as he climbed out the window, grasped the luggage railing, and pulled himself onto the top of the car, which was zipping along at 60 miles per hour. But when a hand suddenly came down over the windshield in front of the driver, everyone noticed!

"A monster!" screamed Art Shamsky, who later became a Cincinnati teammate of Pete's. "A monster from outer space!"

The car screeched to a stop, and the ballplayers leaped out to find Rose sitting on the roof, laughing like a madman.

Then there was the case of the Frogball. This time, however, Rose was an innocent bystander. It seems one of the Macon players was a Venezuelan outfielder who hated frogs. That proved to be quite a problem for him because every time it rained in Macon—which was often—the town was overrun with frogs.

After one rain, Mel Queen (who also later made the Reds) was standing in right field having a between-innings catch with the frog hater, who was over in center field. What the frog hater didn't know was that earlier Queen had taped a frog to a baseball.

Queen wound up and fired history's first and only frogball, and Queen was always noted for having a strong arm. The Venezuelan caught it and . . . splat! "He threw away his glove and started running," recalled Pete with a chuckle. "It took quite a while to get him back in the game."

But even without all the fun and games Rose would have enjoyed that season at Macon. He finished the '62 campaign with an impressive .330 batting average and led the Sally League in runs scored (136) and triples (17).

Rose reported to the Reds for spring training in 1963. But despite his last two excellent seasons in the minors, no one expected him to stick with the big club. Manager Hutchinson, a Rose fan from the beginning, did say, "If I had any guts, I'd stick that kid at second base and forget it." But Rose still seemed destined for more minor league seasoning. He was only 21 and had less than three full seasons of low minor league experience. Besides, the Reds seemed set at second base with veteran Don Blasingame.

"We definitely expected to get Rose sometime before the Reds made their final cuts," said Don Heffner, manager of the Reds' AAA farm team in San Diego.

"All we knew about Rose," said veteran Reds' pitcher Jim Maloney, "was that he had a great year in Macon and had a reputation for running as hard as he could to first base on walks. But it was a long run from Macon to Cincinnati. It was a tremendous jump, and no one really thought he could make it. No one thought he could beat out the Blazer [Blasingame]."

One night in early spring a reporter covering the

Reds handed ten veterans papers and pencils and asked them to list the 25 players they thought would make up Cincinnati's final regular-season roster. Ironically, the only player who listed Rose was Blasingame.

Pete wasn't scheduled to play in the Reds' first exhibition game against the Chicago White Sox in Tampa. He was preparing to go to the clubhouse after a vigorous pre-game workout when Mike Ryba, a minor league manager who had taken a liking to Pete, advised him to hang around the bench on the off chance that Hutchinson might decide to use him later in the game.

Pete hung around, and the game went into extra innings. Every time Hutchinson looked at his bench, he saw the eager rookie on the edge of the seat, staring hopefully back at him. Finally, the manager sent Rose up to pinch-hit.

Pete hit a double, then stayed in the game at second base when the Reds took the field. He came to bat again in the 14th inning, hammered out another double and raced home with the deciding run in a 1–0 victory when the next batter singled. No one knew it then, but Blasingame's days as the Reds' regular second baseman were numbered.

Rose ran wild that spring. Whitey Ford saw him dash to first after drawing a walk and the nickname "Charlie Hustle" was born. "The kid is as hard as this," Hutchinson said, pounding the iron support of the batting cage before a game against the Philadelphia Phils in Clearwater.

"Can he run?" Phils' manager Gene Mauch asked Hutchinson.

"He goes to first in 4.1 seconds," replied the Reds' field boss, "but that's only after he has walked . . . He's everywhere. I see him awake, I see him asleep, and now I see him peeking in bar windows. Rose! Pete Blankin' Rose!"

Hutchinson's mock annoyance scarcely hid the affection he felt for his brash young rookie. Though Hutchinson was known as "The Bear" because of his impressive physical strength and occasional awesome displays of temper, he also had a soft side and was fiercely loyal to his players—as long as they gave him 100 percent. With a youngster like Rose, who gave him the proverbial 110 percent, he became almost fatherly. In return, Rose looked up to his manager with a respect that bordered on reverence. It was a rare relationship in the mostly hard-bitten world of professional baseball.

Despite that close relationship and his fine pre-season showing, Pete wasn't counting on playing in Cincinnati that year. He got his first inkling that he might really make the club after a brief road trip to Mexico City with the Reds. During that trip he managed only two hits in 20 at-bats. Expecting to be benched, he was surprised and delighted that Hutchinson kept him in the starting line-up when the team returned home.

But as the training period drew to a close and the Reds started preparing for the start of the regular season, Rose still hadn't officially been notified that he'd made the major league club. It wasn't until the night before the season opener that Pete could at last relax.

That night he signed his first big-league contract.

Young Pete Rose took risks. Above, he dives back to first ahead of the ball. Below, he grabs a bad throw before being upset by the baserunner. His daring and his bat won him the award as National League Rookie of the Year in 1963 (far right).

After his rookie year, Pete had an eventful off-season. In November he entered the Army Reserves (below), and in January he married Karolyn Engelhardt (right).

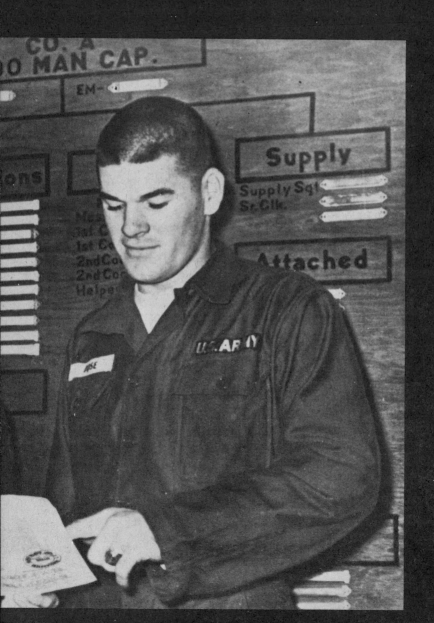

THE
MAJOR
_____ # LEAGUES

"Actually, I wasn't nervous about opening day until just before the game. That's when they brought the whole Rose clan down to get some pictures. My dad was proud as thunder, but I could tell he was nervous, too. My mother posed like a veteran. Then there was the umpire shouting, 'Play ball!' And there I was—in the majors for real."

PETE ROSE

The first Cincinnati batter of the 1963 season was Pete Rose. Pittsburgh pitcher Earl Francis wound up and delivered a pitch. As his father had taught him, Pete followed the ball all the way to the catcher's glove—and immediately got into trouble with umpire Jocko Conlan.

"Listen, you young rookie," the ump growled at Rose, "don't look back here at me. I don't need help with my calls."

Stunned by Conlan's outburst, Pete didn't even try to explain his reflex action. "I was too scared to do anything," he said later. "There were thirty thousand fans up there in the stands watching. I just stood there, waiting and hoping and praying."

Francis threw two more balls and by the third

pitch, the umpire realized that the young Red wasn't trying to show him up. Francis threw a fourth straight ball, and Rose took off on a mad dash for first, earning his first major league hand. Two batters later, Frank Robinson homered for the Reds and Rose scored his first big run.

That was the high point of Pete's debut. Although he did participate in four double plays, he was hitless in his next three at-bats and, to his embarrassment, let a hot grounder sail through his legs for a fielding error.

The next day, however, Rose got his first major league hit. He lined a pitch by Pirate ace Bob Friend down the left-field line, scampered around the bases, and dove head-first into third base for a triple. It seemed he was on his way.

He wasn't. Like most rookies, Rose found himself overmatched by the speed, stuff, and control of big-league pitchers. He promptly went into a slump, getting only two more hits in his next 18 at-bats. In his first road game he struck out four times in a row against Philadelphia's Art Mahaffey. "There's as much difference between major and minor league pitching as there is between day and night," Pete observed.

Rose soon found himself on the bench—but not for long. After giving Pete a brief breathing spell to ease the pressure, Hutchinson put him right back into the starting line-up—this time for good. By the end of

June the Reds were confident enough about Rose's future to sell Blasingame to the American League Washington Senators. "That spell on the bench did me a lot of good," Pete admitted. "I watched the pitchers and saw how they set up the hitters."

Rose's obvious enthusiasm and hustle quickly made him a favorite with the Cincinnati fans. However, he was not as popular with his teammates. Some called him "Hot Dog," convinced that Pete's hustle was simply his way of showing off. Others resented the way he had displaced Blasingame, a popular veteran on the club. And still others didn't like the fact that he was very friendly with the Reds' two black stars, Frank Robinson and Vada Pinson.

"I didn't realize then what was going on," Pete said later. "I didn't know why the other players weren't friendly. Robinson and Pinson at least made me feel at home. And, of course, they were great players I'd admired for years. I was flattered they made me feel a friend of theirs."

"Pete wasn't given Blasingame's job," Robinson explained. "He earned it. He earned everything he ever got. He made people notice him. He did extra things all the time and just hustled his way onto the club."

In time, Rose was accepted by his teammates, who came to realize that the rookie hustled because he wanted to win games—not cheers. And when they saw how good he was and how much he could help the club, Blasingame's departure became easier to take. As for those who didn't like his close association with blacks—Pete didn't much care what they thought.

Rose thought he had learned a lot about baseball in the minor leagues, but his first season in the majors taught him just how much he still didn't know. Fortunately, Fred Hutchinson realized that his 21-year-old rookie was a mere babe in the woods and had Rose room with infielder Daryl Spencer, a wise old baseball veteran. "What that guy didn't know about the game hadn't happened yet," Pete said.

Among other things, Rose had to be warned about the little psychological tricks that rival players tried to pull on inexperienced rookies. Batting against Philadelphia one time, Pete was startled to hear Phils' catcher Mike Ryan say, "Now, Pete, I'm going to tell you what's coming next. Here comes a fastball."

Rose watched and, sure enough, in blazed a fastball. "Aw, shut up, man," Pete said to Ryan. "I don't want to know what's coming."

"Here comes a curve," replied Ryan.

In came a curve ball.

"Listen," Pete said to plate umpire Doug Harvey. "Can't you shut this guy up?"

"Not me," said Harvey. "I can't shut him up."

"Here comes another fastball," chirped Ryan.

Zip.

Rose was so flustered by Ryan's "help" that he

made out two times in a row. However, the third time up, Pete slashed a double despite the catcher's distracting tactics. "The next day he didn't call any pitches when I was batting," Rose said. "He seemed sad about something."

Dodger shortstop Maury Wills tried a different trick on the Reds' youngster early in the season. Pete had just roared into second base with one of his typical head-first slides. As Rose stood up and began dusting off his uniform, Wills said, "Excuse me, Pete," in an ever-so-innocent voice. "I'm going to kick the dirt off the bag."

Pete obligingly began to step off second base. He had one foot off when he suddenly froze. Poised nearby like a vulture was Wills—with the ball. One more step and Pete would have been tagged out in a most embarrassing manner.

Rose's major league education continued on many fronts, although he would be the first to admit that it takes a lot longer than one season to develop real baseball savvy.

Take the seemingly simple matter of when to try to stretch a single into a double. Actually, it isn't simple at all. In the few seconds he has while dashing to first base, a base-runner must take into account the skill of the man fielding the ball. How alert is he? How quickly does he charge a ball? And how strong is his arm? In addition, he must also consider the inning, the number of outs, the score of the game, and the condition of the playing field. "There's a lot more to baseball than just swinging away," Pete observed.

Some of the people Pete was swinging away against that first season were star pitchers like Warren Spahn of the Braves, Juan Marichal of the Giants, and superstar Sandy Koufax of the Dodgers. Koufax, who won 25 games in 1963 and lost only five, gave Rose the most trouble.

Rose considered Koufax one of the greatest pitchers who ever lived. When Pete was a raw rookie, Koufax was a nine-year veteran with two World Series behind him. Sandy was famed for his searing fastball and sharp-breaking overhand curveball. "Only you know how he used to get me out?" Rose said. "He used to get me out on forkballs. I guess I'm one of the few guys he ever threw forkballs to. He'd strike me out and then he'd stand out there on the mound, laughing at me. He got the biggest kick out of doing me that way. But nobody got mad because that's the way baseball is."

Although Rose had a healthy respect for the many pitching stars he faced, he refused to be intimidated by them. "I feel if a hitter is in the groove, if he's swinging his bat good, God could be out there pitching and the batter would still land a solid one," Pete explained. "Then again, maybe the following week the batter isn't grooving and anybody can get him out." Hitting wasn't really Pete's problem, though. It was in the field that he needed help.

" 'Watch the other guys.' That's the advice they hammered at me my first year in the majors. 'Watch how the other guys do it, Pete, and you might pick up a few new tricks,' " Rose said.

Pete took that advice seriously and tried to model himself after Bill Mazeroski, the Pittsburgh Pirates' great veteran second baseman. Mazeroski was one of baseball's smoothest fielders, and Rose would watch him scoop up grounders in pre-game practices by the hour.

Once Mazeroski became aware of the Red rookie's interest, he would give him advice and demonstrate techniques, despite the fact that Pete was an opponent who could conceivably use his improved fielding ability to beat the Pirates.

Rival players frequently used to help each other in those days, a practice that has since been outlawed. Today, just talking to an opponent on the field can result in a fine. "They call it fraternizing—like fraternizing with the enemy—because they feel the public doesn't like to see two teams saying hello to one another," said Rose.

Pete liked to talk to opposing players, he liked to visit their cities, and he liked to play in their ballparks. Most major league players quickly tire of road trips—the fatigue, the endless waiting, the living out of a suitcase, etc. But to Rose, who often said there was *nothing* about baseball he didn't enjoy, each road trip was like a holiday.

After all, seeing the country's biggest cities and most famous ballparks for the first time would be a thrill to any young player, especially one from a small town like Anderson Ferry. Pete visited each new park and simply sat and stared in awe. It was hard to believe he was actually in a place he had only read about or seen on television.

New York particularly fascinated Rose. The Reds used to stay in the Hotel Roosevelt in downtown Manhattan. It was a long bus ride from there to the Polo Grounds in the Bronx where the Mets then played. On the trip to the ballpark, Pete would indulge in one of the ballplayers' favorite time-killing activities—people watching. It always saddened him to see block upon block of decaying tenements as the bus rode through the city's worst slums, but the sights were not always grim and depressing. "I remember one time we were traveling through some pretty ritzy neighborhood where we had seen people walking their dogs and cats on a leash, only there was this one guy and on his leash was a duck! Yeah, New York is a lot different than Sedamsville," Pete said.

Pete Rose was a long way from the Genevas and Macons of the world, in more ways than one. No longer did he face overnight road trips in a station wagon. "We slept sitting up," he said of his minor league days. "In the majors, you're assured of eight hours' sleep before every game . . . and in a bed.

"And we got three-and-a-half dollars a day for

meals in the Sally League. I'd eat a two-dollar breakfast and have a buck-and-a-half left for the rest of the day. I always wound up spending my own money because I've always believed it's important to eat good meals."

In his rookie year in the majors, Rose got ten dollars per day to eat, almost three times his Sally League allotment. He no longer had to spend his own money to eat. "Heck," Rose said, "a guy should hit better in the majors than the minors just because of the improved living and traveling conditions."

Whatever the reason, Pete's game was better than ever. He played in 157 games his rookie season and racked up 170 hits in 603 times at bat for a .273 average. He collected 25 doubles, nine triples, and six homers and scored 101 runs. It all ended up to a fine performance, one that earned him the National League's Rookie of the Year award.

Pete never forgot the day he learned of that great honor. "I was scrubbing the floor of a latrine at Fort Knox, Kentucky," he said with a laugh. "I sloshed some more suds on the floor to celebrate."

DOUBLE TROUBLE: SGT. ROBERT E. LEE & THE SOPHOMORE JINX

"We were all in the same mess together. That's the way we looked at it. Since everybody felt that way, we actually had some fun. But on the other hand, only a nut would admit that being a recruit is a barrel of laughs."

PETE ROSE

All things considered, 1963–64 was not a very good year for Pete. Soon after his rookie season ended, he exchanged the red and white flannels of the Cincinnati Reds for the khaki fatigues of the United States Army. He was assigned to six months' active duty at Fort Knox, Kentucky, to be followed by a three-year period of regular meetings with a Reserve unit in nearby Fort Thomas, just across the Ohio River from Cincinnati.

Because he was a "celebrity," Pete was immediately made a platoon guide, which meant he was a leader among the recruits. But he didn't let his new title go to his head. "I was always one of the guys because I didn't know how to be anything else," Rose said.

Pete's fame did help him avoid one of the more unsettling rituals of military life, however. Soon after they reported to Fort Knox, Pete and his fellow recruits were scheduled to receive their first army "haircut" (actually their heads would be shaved practically bald).

Fortunately for Pete, that evening he was supposed to speak at a sports banquet in town, and the colonel who was taking him there decided he'd rather not deliver a plucked chicken. So while the other 73 new recruits got scalped, Rose was spared. "I'll be honest," he admitted. "That was one moment the guys in my platoon didn't exactly look upon me with favor."

The other recruits were still grumbling as Pete and the colonel set off for town. All went well at the banquet, and by the time it ended Rose and the colonel (who was an avid baseball fan) were feeling like old friends. Colonels, who rank just one step below generals, were seldom seen around the areas in which the lowly recruits were trained, and when they were, they were treated like visiting royalty. So when the colonel's car was spotted near the barracks housing Rose's platoon, everyone, including the company commander, snapped to attention and stayed that way. "Everything was silent," Pete recalled. "You could hear a pin drop."

Out popped Rose, who couldn't resist turning around and, in a voice loud enough to be heard by everyone, shouting, "Hey, thanks, Colonel. I'll see you later, old buddy." The company commander, a stiff, by-the-books lieutenant, did a slow burn. The other recruits, still at attention, had to bite their cheeks to keep from laughing.

Rose saved some of his best stunts for his platoon sergeant, Robert E. Lee. As anyone who has ever gone through basic training will testify, platoon sergeants are rarely known for their sense of humor. Robert E. Lee was no exception, although even Rose admitted that the sergeant "managed to keep his good nature most of the time."

It couldn't have been easy for Lee when you consider some of the pranks Rose and his recruits pulled. "We were, as a platoon, all against our sergeant, and like recruits will do everywhere, anytime we could give him a hard time and get away with it, you can bet your bottom dollar that we did," Rose explained.

One day, for example, Pete and a friend "borrowed" their sergeant's car, rode around in it for a while, then hid it. "We let the poor guy suffer, thinking it was gone for good. Just as he was about to call the military police—or the Pentagon, I'm not sure which because he was real upset—we told him where we had 'seen' it," Rose said.

The recruits were kept on a strict, no-frills diet during basic training. Pete and his cronies tried their best to improve it by sneaking into the PX, buying forbidden goodies, and hiding them in their barracks.

Unfortunately, the sergeant found the stash and the private little grocery store was closed quickly and permanently. Pete soon learned that Robert E. Lee was a hard man to fool. "Everything—well, most everything—we thought up, some other recruit platoon long before we got there had also thought up and tried," Rose said.

Then there was the time platoon guide Pete was marching his men and mistakenly called "Left flank, march!" when he meant "Right flank, march!" Instead of stepping off smartly down the road, the platoon paraded down an embankment and was just about to march into a muddy ditch when Rose shouted "Halt!"

Pete graduated from basic training on January 18, 1964. Exactly one week later, he married Karolyn Ann Englehardt. He had first seen Karolyn at a race track during the 1963 season and been instantly attracted to her. With typical Rose hustle, he'd arranged an introduction and begun dating her. Soon they were going steady, and then they became engaged.

The Roses' marriage did not get off to a very romantic start, however. "We spent our honeymoon in a motel near Fort Knox," Pete recalled. "It wasn't exactly the greatest motel in the world. The bridal suite—which was the same as any other room in the dump—cost four bucks a night. But it had four walls, a ceiling, a television, and a roof. Some honeymoon!"

For the next few weeks Pete helped Sgt. Robert E.
Lee train the next platoon, and then he assisted a
sergeant who coached the Fort's baseball team. A
short while later, his active service ended and he
returned home, a civilian again except for his periodic
Reserve meetings at Fort Thomas.

At Fort Thomas, Pete served as company cook for
the other reserves. He didn't find it particularly
difficult. ("Everything is spelled out in the military
cookbook," he explained.) The biggest problem was
learning to deal with the outlandishly large quantities
a cook has to use when preparing food for hundreds
of men.

The first time Pete had to make iced tea for 120
men, he was a bit uptight and asked a more experienced cook how he should go about it.

"Easy, Pete," the other cook said. "Instead of
putting in two teaspoons of sugar, dump in two
pounds. And lots of luck."

The cook wasn't talking about baseball when he
wished Rose luck, but, as it turned out, that was
where he really needed it. For in 1964 Pete fell victim
to one of the game's classic miseries—the sophomore
jinx.

There are logical reasons to explain the seemingly
mysterious decline many young ballplayers suffer in
their second major league season. For one thing,
there's a natural and unavoidable mental letup once a

man feels he has it made and no longer has to battle for a spot on the roster. For another, by a player's second season, rival pitchers have had a year to observe him, to search out and exploit his weaknesses.

To make things worse, as soon as a player (particularly a young one) starts going bad, he loses confidence quickly. He begins to press and listen to well-meant advice, which more often than not only winds up confusing him. In desperation, he starts to experiment—changing his stance or his grip or his swing—and gets himself even more fouled up. Like a man sinking in quicksand, the harder he struggles to free himself, the deeper he sinks.

For all these reasons, Rose sank like a stone at the start of the 1964 season. He was often benched or used just as a pinch-hitter. His average plummeted to around .200 as he struggled to pinpoint the problem.

Pete knew that there were many possible explanations for his slump. He might be swinging too quickly—or he might be swinging too slowly. He might have begun jerking his head instead of keeping it steady as the pitch came in, or developed some other mannerism that was hurting his timing. Whatever the cause, Pete was prepared to take countless hours of extra batting practice to solve the problem. For help, he turned to Ted Kluszewski, the Reds' batting coach.

But even Kluszewski had no easy answers. First the

coach had Rose try a lighter bat; then he had him try a heavier bat. He had him move closer to the plate; he had him move further away. But nothing seemed to help, and Pete began to worry about being dropped from the club.

While Pete was still in his slump, the Reds made a road trip to Los Angeles, which was located uncomfortably close to Cincinnati's Triple A farm club in San Diego. Pete became more nervous than ever when he began hearing rumors that the San Diego general manager was on his way to L.A., where he'd be picking up a few unfortunate Reds to take back to the minors. The struggling young sophomore spent a few sleepless nights cursing the cockiness that had led him to sign a contract in which he agreed to take a salary cut if he ever got sent back to the minor leagues.

Fortunately Fred Hutchinson wasn't ready to give up on his young second baseman. Pete continued to work on his hitting—but with little success. Finally, with two months gone in the season, Hutchinson called Pete into his office. "I remember it like it was yesterday," Rose said. " 'Pete,' he told me, 'I know you've been trying what we wanted you to do, but it doesn't seem to be working. Go back to the way you were doing it.' "

With that vote of confidence from his manager as well as the encouragement of friends, who, during one game, hung a big sign at the Reds' ballpark,

"Rose Can't Bloom on a Bench," Pete finally began to come out of the doldrums. In a game against Pittsburgh, he hung in there against the Pirates' 6-foot-6, hard-throwing right-hander Bob Veale, fouling off five pitches before finally getting a base hit. "I guess that convinced them I was up there battling because I played the next day," he said.

Rose stayed in the regular line-up for the rest of the season and managed to bring his batting average up to a respectable .269. Still, it was disappointing in view of his .273 rookie mark. His number of games played dropped from 157 to 136, his hits from 170 to 139, his doubles from 25 to 13, his triples from 9 to 2, his RBI's from 41 to 34, and his runs scored from 101 to 64. But what really upset Rose was the fact that the Reds lost the 1964 National League pennant to the St. Louis Cardinals by just one game. He couldn't help feeling that if he had played just a little bit better, the Reds would have made it to the World Series.

Tormented by such thoughts and shaken by the first failure in a career that until then had consisted of a string of solid successes, Pete decided to play winter ball in South America. "I was scared," he explained. "I had just learned that there was an awful lot about baseball that I didn't know."

THE ALL-ROUND PLAYER

Pete learned quickly at Cincinnati, and soon he was a
true triple-threat. At bat he averaged well over .300 . . .

. . . on the bases he ran aggressively, and in the
field he became an all-star second baseman.

THE
EMERGING
STAR

"I had my work cut out for me. I knew if I didn't improve, I might not stay with the majors."

PETE ROSE

It was on a bus ride to Santo Domingo in the Dominican Republic that Rose heard a news report on the radio and learned that Fred Hutchinson had died of cancer. It wasn't a surprise to Pete—he and the rest of the Reds had watched their manager wage a brave but hopeless fight against the disease all season—but it was shocking nevertheless.

"Damn it all anyway!" said Rose years later. "Hutch always tried to help me grow up. He'd talk to me like a father. He'd tell me not to do certain things and that I could make myself a bigger man by not doing them. And he took the good we had with the bad we had and he'd look only at the good in us. Damn it all anyway! Don't you see? He never saw me have a good year, and I owed him that. He's the guy

89

who gave me the chance to be in the major leagues in the first place. It seems like every year since he died I've hit .300, only he never saw me do it."

Ballplayers could earn $1,500 for the brief Latin American winter season, but Pete hadn't come for the money. He had come to improve his game, and judging by his first performance south of the border, there was plenty of room for improvement. In one inning of that game Rose made four errors, and the emotional Latin fans gave him an unmerciful going over.

At first, Rose got so angry that he considered packing up and going home. He didn't mind the booing so much, but when a bottle came flying out of the stands at him, he decided he'd had enough. Instead of quitting, however, Pete drew on an inner reserve and decided no one was going to run him out of town. "Why?" he said. "Because I was growing up a little more, play by play."

He stayed and eventually came to appreciate the enthusiasm of the Latin fans who, in their own way, were a little bit like Rose himself in their all-out commitment to the game. "There's nothing halfway about them," he understated.

There was nothing halfway about Rose, either. He had come to South America to work—and work he did. That winter Pete greatly improved his fielding and even regained his batting stroke. He led the league in runs scored, and his team won the league championship.

Already in excellent shape when he reported to the Reds for spring training in March 1965, Pete sprayed line drives all over the field. He convinced even his harshest critics that Rose had indeed bloomed.

"I thought it was just ballplayer talk when Pete told me how much he had improved as a hitter playing winter ball," said teammate Frank Robinson. "I guess it wasn't."

Dick Sisler, who took over as Reds' manager from Hutchinson, added, "Pete is at least seventy-five percent better in the field than he was a year ago. He makes the double play and he makes the plays to his right. Those are plays which used to give him trouble."

Nothing gave Rose trouble once the '65 season began. Fully recovered from his sophomore slump, he emerged as one of baseball's brightest young stars. In his third year he played in all 162 games and led the National League in times at bat (670) and hits (209). His .312 batting average ranked fifth in the league, and his 117 runs scored ranked third. He also had an impressive 35 doubles (which tied him for third place in the league), 11 home runs, and 11 triples. Finally, he more than doubled his RBI's, from 34 to 81, an outstanding figure for a singles-hitting leadoff man.

That year, he played on his first All-Star team, and Charlie Hustle stories began to spread around the league. Only this time, no one dared make fun of the intensity with which Pete Rose played baseball.

"It took awhile to accept Pete, to see he wasn't trying to show you up," a teammate admitted. "He made you hustle because you were always afraid he was going to run right over you if you didn't. For example, on the basepaths you were always afraid he was going to pass you by. Or after your team made the third out in the field and you were trotting in, you'd hear the sound of running feet behind you and you knew you had better get out of there or Pete would go up one side of you and down the other. He even runs to the shower."

The American League only had to deal with Rose in pre-season, All-Star, and World Series games. But for Detroit Tigers' second baseman Dick McAuliffe, one exhibition game against the Reds in 1965 was enough for him to say, "Pete Rose is the best all-round competitor I've ever seen."

During that game McAuliffe was guarding second base, and Rose was the runner on first. Glancing over, McAuliffe saw Pete casually straddling the bag, apparently absorbed in the action at home plate. Reassured that Rose wasn't running, McAuliffe moved back toward his position between first and second. Suddenly, Rose broke for second, catching the Tiger second baseman flatfooted. McAuliffe was still five feet away from the bag when the catcher's throw bounced off second base and into center field. Rose took third.

In the fifth inning of the same game, Rose was the

lead runner in what should have been a double play. But the usually unflappable McAuliffe, still shaken from their first encounter and now the target of a head-first Rose cross-body block, panicked and threw wild to first.

Roger Maris, the New York Yankee slugging star who was later traded to the St. Louis Cardinals, also learned the hard way that you can't relax for a second when Rose is involved in the play. In a pre-season game against the Yanks, Pete hit a screaming line-drive single to Maris in right field. Figuring the ball was too hard hit for Rose to try for an extra base, Maris tossed the ball in a bit too casually.

That was all Pete needed. Without hesitating for even a moment, he tore around first and belly-whopped into second ahead of the throw from the startled Maris.

Rose once surprised even the great Willie Mays, then in his prime. One day Mays caught a long fly off Pete's bat. As their paths crossed at the end of the inning, Rose yelled to Mays, "Hey, you better play me deeper."

Mays said, "Man, what are you talking about? You can't hit that ball over my head."

The next time up, Rose hit the ball over Mays' head. Later in the game, Mays wound up standing on second base. Looking at Rose, Willie said, "Man, you're not that strong."

Rose smiled and said, "I weigh one ninety."

Mays said, "Hey, damn, you weigh more than me!"

Any skeptics who thought Rose had a lucky year in 1965 had to change their minds by the end of 1966. Playing in 156 games, Pete slammed 205 hits in 654 at-bats to raise his average one point to .313. He hit 38 doubles, 5 triples, and a career-high 16 home runs, a mark he equaled three years later. He drove in 70 runs, scored 97, and again was the starting National League All-Star second baseman.

Even Pete would admit he didn't earn All-Star honors on the strength of his fielding, however. Although he had become an adequate fielder through sheer persistence, Rose never fully mastered the art of making a double play. As a result, he had been tried at third base for 16 games during the '66 season, an experiment that did not work out successfully. So over the winter, Pete's old friend Dave Bristol (by then the new manager of the Reds) made a vital decision for Pete and the team. Excellent young second baseman Tommy Helms, Pete's new roommate, was ready for a regular job, so Bristol decided to put Pete in left field for the '67 season.

"I didn't worry about shifting Pete to left field," Bristol said. "As a second baseman, he charged grounders, he was fast, he had a good arm, and he was good going back on pop flies. If he could do all those things, he could play left field."

The only thing that worried Bristol was how to break the news to his All-Star. The manager gave the problem some serious thought and came up with an unusual solution. During an off-season trip with Pete, Bristol asked him to name the strongest team the Reds could put on the field in 1967. With no hesitation, Pete reeled off a line-up that included Helms at second base. Stopping himself in mid-sentence, he grinned and said, "I guess that puts me in the outfield."

Once he had accepted the idea, Pete approached his new position with typical self-confidence. Asked by reporters during spring training which players he thought he'd have to beat out to become the National League's All-Star left fielder, Rose replied, "They'll all have to beat me out. If I can make the All-Star team as an infielder, I can make it as an outfielder."

Rose had no trouble adjusting to the outfield in '67, even though he was moved from left to right midway through the year. In fact, when he had to fill in at second base for two weeks while Helms was doing army reserve duty, Pete felt out of place. "Pete was so eager to get back to the outfield, he could hardly wait until Tommy got back," remarked Bristol.

"I love the outfield now," said Rose. "I don't feel right at second base any more."

Pete approached outfield play the same way he approached everything in baseball—with all-out, head-first, damn-the-torpedoes abandon. This time, however, he might have been better off with just a bit less hustle. In June, Pete hurt his right shoulder making a diving shoestring catch. Although he seemed stunned at first and just lay in the grass, seconds later he insisted he was all right. But when someone hit a ball to him a little later, he couldn't throw it at all and had to leave the field. He wound up sitting out 14 full games and being restricted to a pinch-hitting role in several others.

Despite the fact that he was named to the All-Star team just as he'd predicted, it was a disappointing season for Pete. Because of the injury, his times at bat fell off to 585, his hits dropped to 176, and his batting average sank to .301.

Pete refused to worry or get down on himself, however. He had successfully made the transition to the outfield, and he felt that if he maintained his health, much better years lay ahead. After all, he was only 26 and already a five-year veteran. He figured to be just entering his prime in 1968.

But even the self-confident Rose never dreamed of the heights he would attain the following two seasons. For at the start of the 1968 season Pete Rose was just on the verge of becoming a true superstar.

BASE HIT # 2,000 FOR PETE ROSE

June 1973 the scoreboard at San ancisco's Candlestick Park announces Pete's newest record. Safe n first base, Pete tips his hat to the owd.

Batting right-handed and left-handed, Pete was one of baseball's most dependable hitters year after year.

THE
BATTING
CHAMPION

"Imagine getting $100,000 for doing what you'd do for nothing!"

PETE ROSE

By the end of the 1967 season Pete Rose was making $46,000 a year, but he thought he deserved much more. "I want to be the first $100,000 singles hitter and prove you don't have to be a home-run slugger to drive a Cadillac," he said. I want players to find out they can make a lot of money just by hitting for average. I don't want guys drifting into other sports just because they don't have a lot of muscle. The clubs have been favoring power hitters. Sure, a home run may be worth four singles. But if the home-run hitter strikes out his next three times up, while the singles hitter gets four hits, that's four runs his team may score instead of one.

"Sure, I'd play this game for nothing if they didn't pay anything. But they pay big, and I want my fair piece of the pie. I think the standards are wrong. Sure the big slugger who produces runs deserves big money. So does the pitcher who wins 20 or 25 or 30 games several seasons running. And so does the guy who collects 200 hits and scores 100 runs year after year. If I can maintain my recent pace, I'll expect to be rewarded for it. The $100,000 is a goal for me, a status symbol."

Rose got off to a poor start in his quest for money and status in 1968. After holding out in the spring until he was offered and accepted a contract for $67,500, he had to overcome a lack of pre-season action with hours of extra batting practice. In the third game of the regular season, he started a 22-game hitting streak that ended when the Philadelphia Phils caught three sizzling Rose line drives. But just when things were really going well, he suffered a disabling injury for the second year in a row. This time he broke his thumb trying to make a shoestring catch in Los Angeles.

The thumb was set and bandaged by Dodger team doctor Robert Kerlan, who became famous for his treatment of outstanding athletes in all sports.

"How long will I be out?" Pete asked Dr. Kerlan.

"An injury like this should keep most athletes out five or six weeks," the doctor replied. "But knowing you, I'd say about three weeks."

The next night Rose insisted on getting into uniform and sitting on the bench. Late in the game he volunteered to pinch-run. "Pete Rose is about the only player I know who would have done that," said Dodger manager Walt Alston, with obvious admiration. "Most players would have watched from the press box or home."

The Reds weren't about to risk a valuable property like Rose pinch-running, however, so they placed him on the 21-day disabled list. In all, he missed 14 games—13 in the regular season plus the All-Star game. He had been the top vote-getter in the All-Star balloting, but his substitute was a pretty fair ball-player, too. Willie Mays took Rose's place in the National League line-up and went on to be named the game's Most Valuable Player. "You made me proud to have you as my sub," Rose said with a grin to Mays in the locker room after the game.

After the All-Star break, Rose grew more and more impatient to get back into action. One rainy afternoon in Pittsburgh, several days before he was due to come off the disabled list, Pete was feeling particularly edgy. Manager Bristol suggested that he and Pete relax with a rubber ball and stickball bat. First Rose pitched up against a wall to Bristol, then Bristol pitched to Rose. Batting left-handed, Pete was surprised to feel no pain in his thumb when he swung.

"Listen," he said to his manager. "I think I'm going to be all right sooner. Why don't I go back to Cincinnati and see the doc?"

"Why not?" replied Bristol.

Rose flew back to Cincinnati and saw team doctors George Ballou and Wally Timmerman. They had

Rose hit a hospital wall with a bat and concluded that while the thumb was not yet fully healed, playing ball wouldn't hurt it.

Rose immediately flew to New York, where the Reds were opening a series against the Mets, and told Bristol the good news. Although he hadn't swung a bat in nearly three weeks, Pete was in the line-up against Met right-hander Don Cardwell. Using a sponge guard for his left hand, Rose went hitless in four at-bats, but he did hit the ball hard twice. The next day he got two hits in four trips to the plate against the great Tom Seaver. Then the Reds traveled to Philadelphia where Pete ripped Phillie pitching for six hits in 16 at-bats. He was back in the groove.

Pete stayed hot, leading the league in hitting by a big margin until a slump in the final weeks of the season allowed Pirate outfielder Matty Alou to close the gap and make the race for the batting championship a dramatic, hotly contested one.

Rose came out of his slump just in time, on the eve of the final weekend of the season. A big factor was the return of his roommate Tommy Helms, who had missed the Reds' final road trip because of a broken wrist. Helms rushed back to Cincinnati from his home in Charlotte, North Carolina, after watching his roomie get only one hit in seven at-bats in a 15-inning game against the San Francisco Giants Friday night, September 27.

"I had to come back so I could get Pete on the

ball," Helms explained. "If what I told him before Saturday's game didn't make him mad, nothing ever will. I told Pete he swung the bat like a girl."

"Tommy's good for Pete," said Bristol. "It's too bad he wasn't on that last trip. When you're in a slump as Pete was, you need a guy like Tommy around. Rooming alone and staring at four walls can drive you batty."

Helms' needling, plus 25 minutes of extra batting practice, helped Pete go 5-for-5 the following day against Gaylord Perry, the Giants' tough right-hander. Rose relaxed, sure he had sewn up the batting title.

"It wasn't until I was standing on second after my fifth hit that I learned Matty went 4-for-4 in Chicago," said Pete. "Hal Lanier told me. I could hardly believe it."

The batting contest wasn't over yet. Rose did some quick arithmetic that night. "Before I went to bed, I had it figured out that I could still win the title if I went 0-for-4 Sunday and Matty went 1-for-4," he recalled. "Of course, that was negative thinking. Bristol wouldn't like that."

The next day, a crowd of 27,464 turned out in Cincinnati to root for Pete in the season finale. That same day, Alou would be making his last try for the crown in a game against the Cubs. Rose himself had mixed emotions. While he was rooting against Alou, he was rooting for the Pirates because a Pittsburgh victory over Chicago would clinch a third-place tie for Cincinnati and mean extra money for each of the Reds.

In his first at-bat, Rose doubled against Ray Sadecki and got a standing ovation. It turned out to be Pete's only hit in three at-bats, but it was all he needed. Alou went hitless in his four times at bat in Chicago, and Rose clinched the title.

"I had a guy posted in the bleachers," Pete revealed after the game. "He must have had a hot-line to Chicago because he told me what Matty did every time he was at bat."

Rose finished the '68 season with a .335 average, three points higher than Alou. His 210 hits tied the Atlanta Braves' Felipe Alou, Matty's older brother, for first place in either league. His 94 runs scored and 42 doubles were both second most in the National League. In addition, he collected 10 home runs, 6 triples, and 49 RBI's.

Rose also helped the Reds in the field. He committed only three errors and led the league's outfielders in assists. "I cut off a lot of runs at home plate," he said proudly.

A few months after the season ended, the balloting for Most Valuable Player in the National League was announced. Rose finished second behind St. Louis Cardinal pitcher Bob Gibson. Speaking with characteristic frankness, Pete let the world know how he felt about missing out on baseball's highest individual honor. "I don't believe a pitcher should be judged on the same basis of votes as an everyday player," explained Rose. "Gibson won twenty-two games for the Cards. I might have won fifty for the Reds.

"When a pitcher has a bad day, forget it. A hitter can have a bad day and help you in the field, at bat with a groundball, on the bases, or with his arm. Gibson's a heck of a pitcher and he had a heck of a year, but he was in thirty-four games and I was in a hundred and forty-nine."

The Reds did ease Rose's disappointment with an $85,000 contract for 1969, however. Pete was rapidly closing in on his goal of becoming baseball's first $100,000 singles hitter.

Rose's bat didn't cool off any during the long winter. He opened the 1969 season with a home run off Dodger great Don Drysdale in his first at-bat, and continued his hot hitting through the early summer months. On August 2, he was batting an impressive .326. But then he went on a real tear, hitting a sizzling .379 in his final 253 at-bats.

By the last week of the season, Pete was locked in another close race for the batting championship, this time with New York Met outfielder Cleon Jones and Pirate outfielder Roberto Clemente, a four-time batting champ and one of the game's greatest stars.

Jones had a few bad days, so it came down to a Rose–Clemente duel. Going into the final game of the season, Pete held a seemingly safe six-point lead.

When a well-meaning friend suggested that Rose play it safe and simply sit out the finale, Pete had a terse two-word reply: "Hell, no."

"It wouldn't have been fair," Rose explained later. "If the situation had been reversed, I wouldn't have wanted Clemente to sit out the last game."

Pete had another reason for wanting to play. He needed just two hits to tie the Cincinnati club record for hits in a season (219 by Cy Seymour in 1906).

Rose was uptight before the game against the Braves in Atlanta. The Braves were starting left-hander Mike McQueen, their 19-year-old rookie. "It's always a little tougher to hit when you're facing a pitcher you've never seen," he explained.

Rose grounded out to the shortstop in his first at-bat, walked in his second, lined to left in his third and grounded into a force out in his fourth. Coming up for his final turn at bat in the eighth inning, he was told by a fan in a front-row box that Clemente had gone 3-for-3 in Pittsburgh. Rose was stunned by the news. "I've never been more nervous in my life than when I went to the plate in that eighth inning," he admitted. "I knew that if Clemente went 4-for-4 and I went 0-for-4, he'd win the title."

There were runners on first and second and the Reds were leading, 5–3, when Rose stepped into the batter's box. With two out, the Atlanta infield was playing back.

The pitch came in and at the last second Pete

squared around and dropped a perfect bunt down the third base line. He smiled and threw his arms up in a gesture of victory as he hit the first base bag safely. He had iced his second straight batting championship.

"That bunt hit was only my fifth of the season—five in six attempts," Rose said later. "It wasn't the longest base hit I've ever gotten, but it has to be one of the biggest. I never ran faster to first in my life. I doubt that any world record-breaking sprinter could have beaten me."

Rose finished the '69 campaign with a .348 average to Clemente's .345. He had 218 hits (one short of the club record), including 33 doubles, 11 triples, and 16 homers. He drove in a career-high 82 runs and scored a career-high 120. He also was named to the league's All-Star fielding team, which proved he contributed with his glove as well as his bat.

Once again he lost out in the ensuing MVP balloting, though, finishing fourth behind San Francisco Giant slugger Willie McCovey. But Rose had two happy moments in the spring of 1970 that more than made up for any disappointment he might have felt at being overlooked again. First, the Reds offered him a contract for $105,000, fulfilling his long-time ambition to reach the salary plateau.

"Pete has proved his worth to our team," said general manager Bob Howsam. "He has set a fine example by his style of play. It proves that an individual doesn't necessarily require size or have to be a home-run hitter to earn an outstanding salary, although it takes a tremendous amount of work. He deserves his milestone contract."

"Usually, players prefer to keep their salaries secret," said Rose with a grin, "but I want the whole world to know about this."

Pete's second big moment, only slightly less thrilling to Pete, was his spring training meeting with Ted Williams, baseball's last .400 hitter and the man many experts consider the greatest batter of all time. "It was the first time I'd ever seen him in person," said Rose, as excited as a Little Leaguer.

"Do you know what he told me? He told me I could be the next .400 hitter . . . that it was possible because I switch-hit, make good contact, and can run. He said it was possible, but I just can't believe it. Why I'd have to get at least 250 hits, going to bat more than 600 times the way I do each year. Now if I only went to bat 400 times, I'd say it was possible. Heck, I've hit at a .400 clip over a two-month span. But a full season, more than 600 at-bats . . .

"I just don't think it's possible."

ROSE AND THE REDS

The most important members of the 1970 Big Red Machine pose on a tractor just before the World Series. They are, left to right, Bobby Tolan, Johnny Bench, Tony Perez, Lee May and Rose.

Johnny Bench and Pete Rose talk to reporters after the Reds beat the Mets in the first game of the 1973 league playoffs. Below, Pete is congratulated by the Reds after his twelfth-inning homer in game four.

ROSE
AND
THE BIG
RED
MACHINE

"I want to win a World Series before I'm through. What ballplayer doesn't?"

Pete wasn't the only Cincinnati player to wield a big bat. In the early '70s the Reds boasted a powerful line-up that included such super-sluggers as Johnny Bench, Joe Morgan, Tony Perez, Lee May, and Bob Tolan. In fact, the Cincinnati batters were so impressive that they became known as the Big Red Machine.

Yet despite their obvious talents, the one great frustration that plagued Rose and his teammates from the time Pete first joined the Reds in 1963 was their inability to win a world championship. The Reds came close twice, winning National League pennants in 1970 and 1972; but for some reason they were unable to capture baseball's biggest prize.

The 1970 Series was no contest, as the Reds were

crushed by the Baltimore Orioles, four games to one. However, their 1972 loss to the Oakland A's was one of those agonizingly close affairs that lingered for months in the minds of the losers.

After losing three of the first four games by scores of 3–2, 2–1, and 3–2, the Big Red Machine rallied and won the next two games to tie up the Series. Heartened by their dramatic comeback the Reds confidently took the field for the crucial seventh game at Cincinnati's Riverfront Stadium. But it proved to be a monstrous anticlimax for the Reds and their fans. The A's squeaked by with a 3–2 victory when Oakland catcher Gene Tenace got a fluke single—on a grounder that took a freakish bounce off the infield Astroturf—and drove in the Series-winning run.

"Damn, I wanted to win this one as bad as any game I've ever played," said a frustrated Rose after the game. Pete had not distinguished himself in either World Series, hitting .250 against Baltimore and .214 against Oakland. Very rarely did he fail to come through in the clutch, so his sub-par World Series performances were especially hard to take.

Despite such disappointments, the Big Red Machine remained a close-knit unit, thanks largely to the leadership of Pete Rose. As one of his first official acts, manager Sparky Anderson (Bristol's successor) had named Pete team captain in 1970. Pete took that job seriously, the way he took everything in baseball.

It was a tribute to Rose that the Reds never broke

into cliques—a common problem on many teams. With the emergence of young catcher Johnny Bench as the team's most glamorous star in 1970 many outside observers had predicted conflicts. When a team has two players of the caliber of Bench and Rose, it can cause problems. Jealousy, division, and dissension often result if a team splits into rival camps, each clustered around one of the superstars.

But instead of being jealous of each other, Rose and Bench became close friends. They even went into business together for a while as co-owners of an automobile agency, bowling alley, clothing stores, and other interests under the name "RBI" (Rose-Bench, Inc.). Eventually the partnership was dissolved when their various businesses failed to make enough money, but the friendship held fast.

"Pete has had a great influence on me," said Bench. "He's beautiful. He befriended me when I first came up, and he set a good example for me both on and off the field. On the field, he always gives it everything he has. Off the field, he's also ambitious and energetic. He loves baseball, and he can't sit still. That's me, too. He's married and has a home and children, while I'm still single and enjoying the swinging bachelor life, so there are times we go our own ways, but we're very close."

And Rose said, "We complement each other. We help each other make money and win games. On the field, I get on base, and Johnny gets me in. He can do things I can't do, and I can do things he can't do. I know someday, because he is a home-run hitter, he'll surpass my salary. I can understand that. I can live with that. Off the field, there were places we thought we could make money together, putting our names together, than we could separately. We have the same financial adviser. We're a good team."

Of course, Pete's main business remained baseball. As he had thought, batting .400 proved to be beyond his and everybody else's reach, but hitting .300 (itself a rarity in baseball's modern era) became routine for Pete. He hit .316, .304, and .307 from 1970 through 1972, collecting 205, 192, and 198 hits.

Then, in 1973, Rose enjoyed the greatest year of his career. He racked up 230 hits in 680 at-bats (tops in both leagues). Ignoring the aches that begin to plague a ballplayer as he enters his 30s, including a painful thigh injury early in the season, Rose played 160 games.

"Pete was really hurtin'," said manager Anderson. "I've seen many a guy with a lot less pain who wouldn't have been playing."

For a change, Pete won the batting title easily with a blazing .388 average. It was his third National League batting crown and his ninth straight .300-plus season. The hustle, dedication, and sheer hard work Pete displayed that year left even hardened professionals bubbling like fans.

"If Pete gave the Reds any more than he does now,

we'd have to take blood from him," said Cincinnati coach Alex Grammas. "I've never seen a guy like him. There's nothing negative about Pete. He's a positive thinker . . . always."

At mid-season, someone had asked Anderson if he thought Rose could be caught in the race for the batting title. "Nobody will catch him," the manager had replied emphatically. "You wanna know why? Because there isn't another player in the league who grinds every day the way Pete does. I mean grinds for 162 games. That's why the old-time ballplayers like Pete. He reminds them of themselves. He doesn't waste time bitching. He's too busy playing baseball.

"Ever watch Pete after a pitcher gets him out?" Anderson asked with a grin. "He'll cross the diamond right in front of the pitcher. He'll yell, 'You ain't got nothing,' at him and he'll add, 'I'll get you the next time.' He'll yell it right into their faces.

"Let the pitcher get mad if he wants to. Let him throw at Pete. That just makes Pete more determined to get a hit."

Two of Rose's 230 hits in 1973 were special. In a game against the Giants in San Francisco on June 19, he rifled a single to center field against Ron Bryant for his 2,000th career hit. When he bounced a ground-rule double over the left-field fence two innings later, Anderson joked, "He sure didn't waste any time starting after the next 1,000."

Naturally, Rose was asked after the game about the

possibility of getting 3,000 hits, a goal he had often mentioned. "I really don't like to think about my 3,000th hit," he said, "because when I get close to it, it'll mean my playing career will be nearing an end."

Rose's second super-hit came on September 17. He slashed a double and a single off Dave Roberts of the Houston Astros, giving him a total of 220 hits for the season to break Cy Seymour's 68-year-old Cincinnati team record. Although he was elated at owning the record, Pete's joy was somewhat dampened by the fact that the Reds lost the game, 5–2. (The Reds had had two runners on base in the ninth when Rose hit into a force play.)

"I just wished I could have gotten that double in the ninth inning instead of the first," he said later. "If I had, we might still be out there playing."

Fortunately, the loss didn't really hurt the Reds. Later that month they clinched the National League West division title, beating out the Los Angeles Dodgers by three-and-a-half games. Although they had been ten-and-a-half games out of first place at one point in the season, the Reds finished with a 99–63 record, the best in either league.

Now only the New York Mets, the East division champs, stood between the Reds and another crack at the World Series. The Mets had finished only three games over .500 at 82–79, and they seemed no match for the Big Red Machine.

As expected, the Reds won the opener, but then the

Mets bounced back with a 5–0 victory in game two. Early in game three the Reds began to realize that 1973 again might not be their year when, to the delight of the 53,967 Met fans assembled in Shea Stadium, New York scored one run in the first inning, five in the second, one in the third, and two in the fourth.

The Reds were trailing 9–2 in the top of the fifth when Rose singled with one out. Rose was frustrated as he rounded first base and ducked back to the base. He never liked to lose, and he found it doubly galling to be so far behind the Mets, a club hardly known for its hitting. And of course this was no ordinary game but one that figured to go a long way toward deciding the National League pennant.

So when Joe Morgan, the next Reds' batter, hit a sharp infield grounder, Rose barreled hard into second in an attempt to break up a double play. Met shortstop Bud Harrelson made the pivot and fired to first to complete the double play a second before Rose crashed into him.

"You . . . you tried to elbow me!" screamed the normally mild-mannered Met shotstop.

"What are you talking about?" shouted Rose, pushing Harrelson hard at the same time.

In an instant, the two men were rolling around the dirt swinging at each other. Players from both benches and both bullpens raced out onto the field and an incredible free-for-all began.

Finally, order was restored on the field, but the trouble was far from over. Angered at the sight of the 5-foot-11, 200-pound Rose pummeling their 5-foot-9, 145-pound shortstop, the Met fans greeted Rose with a shower of beer bottles, paper, fruit, and soft drink cans when the Reds outfielder attempted to take his defensive position in the next inning. When a heavy whiskey bottle whizzed by Rose's head, Cincinnati manager Sparky Anderson decided he'd seen enough. "That does it!" Anderson yelled to umpire Chris Pelekoudas. "I'm pulling my team off the field until you get this solved. I don't want anybody hurt."

The departure of the Reds from the field seemed to further enrage the crowd. A full-scale riot and a Met forfeit began to loom as definite possibilities. Finally, National League president Chub Feeney asked Met manager Yogi Berra to lead a delegation of Mets onto the field in an attempt to calm the crowd. Berra, Willie Mays, Cleon Jones, Tom Seaver, and Rusty Staub walked all around the huge park holding their hands up in gestures of peace. It worked, and a potentially dangerous, destructive scene was averted. The game continued and the Mets maintained their 9–2 lead for their second playoff win.

In game four, the teams were locked in a 1–1 tie when Rose homered in the twelfth inning to give the Reds their second victory. But the Mets' decisive 7–2 victory in the fifth and final game ended Cincinnati's dream of a world championship. The Big Red Machine had run down, and Pete's great season ended on a sour note.

Rose didn't want to get his hopes up too high when the time for the announcement of the MVP award approached. That made it doubly sweet when the news came out later that year. In the balloting of the Baseball Writers of America, Pete edged out Pittsburgh Pirate slugger Willie Stargell (who led the major leagues in home runs and RBI's) for the title. A telling blow had been struck for singles hitters everywhere. One of their own had been judged more valuable than all the game's musclemen and pitchers.

But Pete's troubles were far from over. The following season (1974) he became the target of the fans' wrath during the Reds' first trip to Los Angeles. Apparently, the Dodger fans had not forgotten the Rose–Harrelson incident—or the fact that the Reds had taken the West division title from L.A.

Pete was showered with debris from the stands, including ice, a rock, and big hunks of wood. Insults far more vile than usual were hurled at him. Only the threat of forfeiture, announced over the public address system and flashed on the scoreboard, finally calmed the crowd. "Baseball isn't fun when you have to go through something like this," said a shaken Rose, his first admission that he had found something less than perfect about the game.

Understandably, the Reds' and Mets' officials were worried about Rose's first 1974 appearance in New

York. Before the Reds arrived, Harrelson himself begged the Met fans to behave. He insisted that he had no hard feelings toward Rose and that, in fact, he greatly admired the Red's fiery competitiveness. And just to make sure there was no more trouble, the Mets beefed up their Shea Stadium security force and kept the outfield section of seats nearest to Rose empty.

Fortunately, those precautions turned out to be unnecessary. The Met fans gave Pete a standing boo and waved banners written especially for the occasion ("Pete Rose Can Kiss My Toes"), but it was mostly good-natured and Pete knew it. He waved back at the fans, and everyone's thoughts returned to baseball. "New York has great fans," concluded Rose.

In the third playoff game against the Mets in 1973, Pete slid hard into
Bud Harrelson to break up a double play and came up with a fight. At
first it's a stand-off (left), but soon Rose gets the upper hand.

At left, Pete and Joe Morgan come in from the outfield the inning after the Harrelson fight, complaining that fans are throwing things at them. The fan with the sign has his say, too. Above, Rose and Harrelson meet weeks later at a banquet and Met manager Yogi Berra keeps peace.

ROSE
ON
HITTING

"I never drive by the ballpark without looking to see which way the flag is blowing. I guess I'm thinking baseball all the time."

PETE ROSE

Pete Rose did not hit .300 for nine straight seasons and win three batting titles by accident. Like most good hitters, he made a study of the art of consistently meeting the ball solidly, something that many experts consider the single toughest athletic skill of all. Hitting a baseball involves a round surface striking a round surface, so the point of contact is extremely small. To connect solidly with a fastball moving more than 90 miles per hour or a sharply breaking curve is a skill far more sophisticated than, say, throwing a block or making a jump shot.

Rose could—and did—talk about hitting for hours on end. "I concentrate on making contact with the ball," he said. "I swing hard, but I don't overswing. I want to be aggressive, but I'm not trying to overpower the ball. I hold the bat still before swinging, and when I swing I try for a level swing. I try to get good wood on the ball. I hit it where it's pitched. If it's inside, I go to the near field with it. If it's outside, I go to the far field with it. I never try to pull the ball, even though it's a temptation in some parks with close fences down the line. I guess the last pull hitter to win a batting title was Ted Williams, but he was something else."

Pete never tried to become a home-run king. To him, getting on base was always the name of the game. "There are only a few fellows who hit for average today and take a run at 200 hits every year," he said. "Years ago, there were a lot of them. The woods were full of .300 hitters. You hit .375 and you maybe still didn't win the batting title. Today you hit .375 and they'll bronze you and make a statue out of you. There seldom are five guys who hit even .300 in each league. I guess it started with the light bats and even small, skinny guys swinging hard for the fences, looking for the home runs. Sure, they surprised a lot of people with the number of homers they hit, but they didn't hit much else. They became bad hitters, they wasted themselves.

"I'm not a bad-ball hitter. I try to swing only at pitches that are over the plate. But I don't walk as much as I might because the pitchers aren't as afraid of throwing a strike to me as they are to a home-run hitter. However, I'll take my walks. Any way I can get on satisfies me.

"The batters who hit for average today hit the ball where it's pitched and hit to all fields. Make contact and you've always got a chance for a hit. Most of the time I try to hit the ball up the middle. That's where the biggest opening is. I didn't realize how big that opening was until I got hurt and watched some games from the press box. It doesn't look as big when you're at the plate because you've got the pitcher standing in front of you. But if you hit the ball right back at him, the chances are it'll get past him because he usually won't be quick enough to pick off a hard-hit ball at that distance.

"Being a switch-hitter gives me an edge. Those sliders and curves are always coming in, not going away. And when I hit the ball left-handed, I'm a step or two closer to first base. I'd hit more homers if I weren't a switch-hitter. Mickey Mantle was an amazing home-run hitter for a switch-hitter. Usually you have more power from one side than the other, and you develop more power by batting consistently from one side. I've been switching since I was nine and still have more power from the right side. But if I were swinging for home runs, I'd have a lot more than I do.

"Even though I'm not a home-run hitter, I consider myself a power hitter because the real way to judge power hitters is on total bases. Either by hitting the ball into the open parts of the outfield or by stretching hits, I usually wind up among the league leaders in doubles and triples, so often I am higher than some home-run hitters in total bases. I drive in my share of runs and score more than my share. If you produce runs, it doesn't matter how you do it."

To make sure he kept producing, Pete took excellent care of his body. "I keep myself fresh," he said. "I sleep until twelve, one o'clock in the afternoon. I don't walk around much days—I save my legs. I go easy on the movies and television to save my eyes. In the summer you never see me sitting by the side of a pool much. Sitting in the sun all day takes the strength out of you. And none of that hamburger stuff for me. I eat good, thick steaks. I keep my strength up, but I let it all out on the field. I don't try to save myself there. I never admit to myself I'm tired. When the other guys are slowing down, I'm coming on."

Fully aware that it was important to be prepared mentally as well as physically, Rose stressed the importance of bearing down all the time. To him, every at-bat was equally important. "You hear guys say, 'We'll get that pitcher out of there after we've seen him once,' " Rose explained. "Or they'll say, 'It's still twilight. You can't see the ball good.' I say this: The time to get the pitcher is right away, before he's loosened up. And in twilight, you should be bearing down harder, when the pitcher has the advantage.

"I'm trying just as hard the fifth time I come up. You're 3-for-4, some guys are satisfied. Not me. You get that fourth hit, you're 4-for-5. Let me show you

how important that one hit can be. Say the next day
you go 0-for-5. That makes you either 3-for-10 for the
two games, which is .300, or 4-for-10, which is .400.
That's 100 points difference. A writer once told me
Stan Musial went after a hit his first time up, then
another and another. That's my system, too. As many
hits as I can get.

"Suppose I go 0-for-2. Some guys get discouraged
and let up. Not me. Billy McCool says he has never
seen anyone go 0-for-2 as often as I do and end up
3-for-5 in a game. Suppose we're ahead 9–1. You
know that pitcher isn't trying as hard as if this were a
2–1 game. That's the time the hitter should bear
down. That's the time he's going to get base hits.

"I'm bearing down every time I come up, even if
we're way behind or way ahead, no matter what I did
the last time up. Every time up is a new chance. It's
not easy. Not physically and not mentally. I know
that. It's easy to say it, but not to do it. You play 162
games, maybe 200 counting exhibitions, you come up
600, 650 times a season, you play night after night
after night with sometimes no day off for a week or
two. It's hard to bear down every time. To the fan
who goes to a game only once in a while, he can't
understand why the player isn't all-out all the time.
But the fan isn't all-out all the time in what he does in
life."

Every batter, even one as consistent as Pete, has
days—and even weeks—when nothing seems to go

right. Just as he did with every other aspect of the game, Rose made a careful study of the batting slump.

"You're going to have slumps," he said philosophically. "Everyone has them. You'll get some bad breaks on well-hit balls, for example. You have to avoid the 0-for-20 slumps. You have to shrug off the bad breaks.

"Sometimes a knuckleball or a screwball pitcher will get me going into a slump because when they pitch that way they get me lunging at the ball. Slumps are funny things. You can be hitting .400 and go into a slump, just like that. I think, though, that most slumps are psychological. Guys start thinking they're in a slump and pretty soon they are because they actually thought themselves into one. But you've just got to remember that sometime in the season you're going to go 0-for-8 or 0-for-10. Whether you want to or not, you will anyway. No one bats a thousand.

"When you're in a slump, any pitcher can get you out. You have to hang in there and keep working. On the other hand, when you get hot, you can hit anyone. I don't care who it is out there—if I'm hot, I'll hit him."

During Rose's second-year slump, he experimented with his stance and swing, which only made the slump worse. That taught him a lesson he never forgot. "I don't fool around with my stance," he said. "I don't take advice from a lot of people. The only person I take advice from is Ted Kluszewski, our batting coach. He's good. He knows me and my style. I trust him. Listening to too many guys just mixes you up. If I'm in a slump, I may move around in the batter's box some, but I won't change my stance or my style. I just try harder at what I'm doing."

Happily, Pete also learned that a hitter often comes out of a slump as suddenly—and unexplainably—as he gets into one. After leading the league in batting for most of '68, for example, he went into a particularly disheartening slump near the end of the season. But then, just as he was getting a little bit desperate, Pete had one of his best days ever. Batting against Giant ace Gaylord Perry, he got five hits in five at-bats.

"It was just one of those days," Pete explained after the game. "It was unbelievable. I hit every one of them on the nose. I felt that if I came up to bat fifty times, I would have got fifty hits. The night before, I felt if I'd come up fifty times, I'd have got just one hit. It was just a complete opposite feeling from what I'd had in the game the night before. As Perry said later on the air, the harder he threw, the harder I hit him."

Strangely enough, Pete often did his hottest hitting against the league's toughest hurlers. "Some guys are scared by the big pitchers," he said. "I'm not. I know they're better than the other pitchers. But every time I go to bat I see at least one good pitch. Even the good ones have to throw you one good pitch. If you don't hit it, you're up the creek, but I always figure I'll see one good pitch. Sometimes I'd rather face the big pitchers than the bad ones or the new ones. Sometimes when I don't know what to expect from a pitcher I may go for a bad pitch and strike out. If I strike out only sixty-five times a year and the other guy strikes out a hundred times, I've had thirty-five more chances to get a hit than he has."

And Pete Rose was always the kind of ballplayer who knew how to make the most of every chance.

Pete gets together with fellow all-stars Larry Bowa and Ron Cey before the 1974 All-Star game . . .

. . . hands an autographed ball up to a young fan during spring training (left), and meets the press after an important game.

Even in the off-season, Rose is a competitor. Here he plays basketball with his Cincinnati teammates.

THE
FANS'
FAVORITE

"I was a kid once myself. I can still remember how thrilled I was when I had a chance to meet a major leaguer, and I can remember, too, how disappointed I was when I asked a player for an autograph and he refused."

Pete Rose was as enthusiastic off the field as he was on it, another reason for his great popularity with his fans. Rose never turned down a request for an autograph. He kept a stack of autographed photos in his locker and took some with him whenever he left the dressing room. When a youngster asked him for an autograph, Pete would give him a signed photo. If he didn't have any photos with him, he would patiently sign a piece of paper. And he'd keep on signing as long as the fans kept asking. Unlike many major leaguers, Rose never forgot that it was the fans who ultimately paid his salary.

"I feel i'm very lucky," he said. "Most guys who fooled around the way I did in high school don't wind up making $100,000. And without baseball, I wouldn't be. And without fans, there would be no baseball. They pay the way, and that's something no player should forget."

One Rose habit that made him a favorite of the fans was the way he always threw back the foul balls that bounced out of the stands. He had been doing it for a long time and even risked the wrath of the Reds' front office to continue the practice. The Reds threatened to deduct the price of the balls from his pay, but Pete continued chucking the ball to the fans anyway.

"You'd be surprised how many people want a game ball," Pete explained. "This is the only game I know where a guy will pay a hundred bucks for a seat in the hopes he'll get his hands on a three-dollar baseball. They simply have got to have that baseball."

Rose's interest in winning friends for the game he loved extended into the off-season, too. He made many personal appearances for the Reds in the winter, and for many years he played on the Cincinnati Reds' basketball team.

"We have to sell baseball in the wintertime," he explained. "Too many guys don't want to do that. When the season ends, the gloves shouldn't be tossed into the corner. There's more to it than that. You can only help yourself. I believe every player should meet as many people as he can, in sports and out of sports, because when a person knows you he's gonna want to go to the park, see you play, and root for you."

No doubt Pete's three biggest fans were his wife Karolyn, his daughter Fawn (born 1964) and son Pete, Jr. (1969). The Roses lived in a luxurious home in suburban Cincinnati that had two fireplaces decorated with the three silver bats Pete won for his batting titles, the Golden Glove he won for his fielding, and numerous other mementoes of his distinguished career.

The young Roses showed their father's influence at an early age. From the time he could walk, Pete, Jr. (nicknamed "Corky") was constantly at Riverfront Stadium, in the clubhouse or swinging at whiffleballs thrown by his dad in the batting cage, pounding out mini line drives. He batted lefty exclusively, but you can be sure his father planned to make him a switch-hitter before long.

Red manager Sparky Anderson recalled the time that three-year-old Pete, Jr., was on the bench before a father-and-son game: "The boy said to me, 'Sparky, when the crowd comes, I play.'

"I said, 'Corky, you're just like your dad.' "

In 1973, when daughter Fawn was in the third grade, she went to the West Hills Country Club where she was introduced to a University of Cincinnati tennis player named Steve Kramer, who was conducting a clinic.

"My daddy's Pete Rose," said the young girl.

"Never heard of him," Kramer joked.

"You know my daddy," insisted Fawn, going into

an excellent imitation of her father's batting stance. "Nope, never heard of him," insisted Kramer.

"He runs the bases like this," said Fawn, taking off down the court and diving head-first into the dust while Kramer and everyone else watching broke up.

Of course, Pete's first fan had been his father, Harry Rose. From the sandlots to the majors, he cheered Pete on. But on December 10, 1970, at the age of 58, Harry Rose died on the front steps of his home when a blood clot reached his heart.

"I didn't know what to think," Pete said. "I had never been through anything like this, and I just could not believe that it was happening to me. You know, other people die—but not your father. I never knew much about death, so I wasn't prepared for it. My father was the most important guy in my life.

"I'm thankful that Dad got the opportunity to see me play and succeed. He saw me play for the Reds and help win a league championship. He saw me win two batting titles, get 200 hits and make the All-Star team. And I'm particularly glad to know that he saw something else. He and I attended a dedication ceremony out in Sedamsville. It was at Bold Face Park, where I started out in Knot Hole baseball and where Dad had played sandlot ball as a kid. They renamed Bold Face Park. It is now called Pete Rose Park. They renamed it after me, and I'm honored. But they should have named it after my dad."

By the end of the 1974 season, Pete's twelfth in the

major leagues, he was 34 years old. That's an age when a ballplayer starts to realize that his career can't last forever. As he reached his mid-30s, Rose was realistic about the future, but hopeful that hard work and heredity would prolong his playing days.

"You know I'm going to keep myself in shape," he said. "And the older I get, the more I'm going to work to keep trim. I just hope I'm like my dad. Remember, he was playing semi-pro football at the age of 42, and that's the toughest kind of play.

"How many more seasons can I play regularly— five, six, seven, eight? I may be able to keep going until I'm close to 40. I'd like to play 15, 16, 17, 18 seasons in all. I'd like to play 20. And I'd like to play the rest of my big league career with the Cincinnati Reds. I want to be the guy who played his whole career in the majors on his hometown team and then went on to become manager of it. I know managing's tough, often a frustrating and unrewarding job, but I'd like to take a crack at it. I think I'd be good at it. I have this feeling for winning. When my legs go, my desire will still be high. It'd be a way to stay close to the game for a while. And I'd consider it even while I was still playing, though it's not the best way."

If Rose did wind up as manager of the Reds, it would be just another of many firsts in his distinguished Cincinnati career. He was the first Red to be both an All-Star infielder and an All-Star outfielder. He was the first Red to win back-to-back batting titles, the first hometown boy to be named team captain, the first Red to earn $100,000. But if it should all suddenly end—if tomorrow Rose was traded—he would have no regrets and feel no bitterness. "I would just pat Mr. Howsan on the back and have no hard feelings," Pete said. "I'd just say that I had enjoyed my stay with the Reds."

Certainly, if Pete never played another game in Cincinnati, he would have already left his mark. For Red fans will always remember Pete Rose . . . the man who holds the team record for games played, at-bats, runs, hits, doubles, total bases, head-first slides, and dirty uniforms . . . the man who seems sure to be elected to the Hall of Fame the first year he's eligible . . . the man they call "Charlie Hustle."

INDEX

Page numbers in italics refer to photographs